A STUDY OF LIBERTY

A STUDY OF

LIBERTY

Horace M. Kallen

GREENWOOD PRESS, PUBLISHERS
WESTPORT, CONNECTICUT

JC
585
.K26
1973

The Library of Congress has catalogued this publication as follows:

Library of Congress Cataloging in Publication Data

Kallen, Horace Meyer, 1882–
    A study of liberty.

    1. Liberty. I. Title.
[JC585.K26 1973]   323.44   72-7964
ISBN 0-8371-6554-7

To Adelbert Ames, Jr., and John Dewey
in glad and grateful remembrance
of their lives and labors

CONTENTS

FOREWORD

Milennia ago, Socrates set a philosophic fashion. Human beings, he averred, could know themselves, they could not know the world wherein their selves lived and moved and had their being. Let them, therefore, not strive to inquire into universal nature. Let them rather examine their own lives, their ends and means with their rights and wrongs and goods and evils. Plato and Aristotle took the Socratic precepts for directives. They, and their medieval and modern epigons, pursued their own inquiries along the Socratic gradient, making cosmology and metaphysics into extensions of ethics, translating the onflowing stream of events which we designate as nature, into a simple, unmoving, self-contained and self-containing universal logic of discourse. They assigned it eternally foregone conclusions, always and everywhere, the same. They personified it as the Logos or Reason, and brought the protean diversity of the flux of experience into conformation with the unity, universality, and eternity wherewith they endowed their magic Word. When, at long last, inquiry found that this was but idolizing a tool, that it had no need for the anthropopathic hypothesis, it nevertheless retained the qualities men had endowed logic with, assigning them now to matter. "Philosophy" wrote Galileo in *Il Saggiatore,* "is written in that great book which lies ever before our eyes—I mean the universe—but we cannot understand it if we do not first learn the language and grasp the symbols it is written in. This book is written in the mathematical language, and the symbols are triangles, circles, and other geometrical figures, without whose help it is impossible to comprehend a single word of it; lacking it, one wanders in vain through a dark labyrinth."

Soon Spinoza undertook to account not only for the universe, but for mankind as well, *more geometrica*. He transposed man's independent examination of himself à la Socrates into an activity dependent upon his discovery and knowledge of the nature which generates him, and which sustains him in the struggle to go on struggling that is his existence. Spinoza called his revolutionary inversion of the Socratic prescription, *Ethics*. From his initiative has developed the tradition of whatever is un-Socratic in modern philosophy. It is a tradition at once challenging, and accounting for, the *philosophia perennis* which stems from Socrates, by measuring the actual contributions of its avatars to the freedom, safety, and happiness that mankind keep struggling in ever greater abundance to achieve. This new tradition proceeds from the belief that mankind can and must know nature if they are reliably to know themselves. The endeavor to know nature which ensues, together with its findings, its ways and works, we call science. In the records of science, earlier findings give way to later ones; what had been appraised as truth becomes reappraised as error; scientific ways and works ongoingly evoke new symbols, new tools, new concepts. These fall into sequent patterns which conjointly compose the tradition of scientific method.

One of the transforming consequences of science

and the scientific method is the industrial economy which incarnates them in new folkways, mores, and value systems. Together, they constitute modernity, and provide the human being the differentiae that qualify him as modern man. Another consequence is the event that while human nature, its career and destiny, are now seen in the perspectives of physics, biology, cosmology, and astronomy, the logic of discourse is demoted from the Logos or Reason of the metaphysician into a passing creation of a human nature struggling for a survival which is but one diversification among the struggles all nature manifests, with its changes and chances, its incalculable spontaneities engendering and ending its calculable necessities. The logic is now recognized as an organ and instrument of mankind's struggle for existence. It is frequently appraised as a calculation of risks postulated on accepting the spontaneities and instabilities of the course of natural events, endeavorings to map and predict and manage them, but unable to account for their "ultimate" *what* or *whence* or *whither*.

Those "ultimates" present themselves as ineffable. They pass on, one after the other, in an interminable succession wherein none need be a beginning, none an end. If one is so qualified, it is by some inquirer's choice shutting out what has preceded, or by his decision cutting off what is succeeding. However the logic of discourse is worked, its outcome is "ultimately" some ineffable inwardly ambiguous; is "ultimately" a process which the words "indeterminate", "liberty", "freedom" point to. Discourse may identify such as ineffable as Spinoza identified his substance, his *nature naturans,* which he also called God; and it may envision its inwardness of freedom as Spinoza envisioned it. Again discourse may identify such an ineffable freedom as Bergson identified his *durée reele,* his *élan vital,* which Bergson also called God, and it may envision the inwardness of that freedom as a creative evolution, forever bringing forth the new. Yet again, discourse may identify such ineffables as do physicists and cosmologists of our day, designating them waves, particles, and indeterminancies; and the inwardness of freedom they envision may at last be another seeing of what the ancients saw as "the declination of the atoms."

Be the stuff of the ineffable a manifold protean elusiveness or an ever-present but hidden unity, its "freedom" is sometimes identified with an ungrounded necessity whence all happenings follow inevitably, and sometimes with a groundless spontaneity whence necessities follow as repetitions and habits of following, so that what we call "effect" is believed not only to follow but to follow *from* what is called "cause." Philosophers argue that one or the other such freedom must pertain to man. Those who consider it ungrounded necessity adjudge groundless spontaneity, indeed any kind of spontaneity, an illusion. Those who consider freedom groundless adjudge ungrounded necessity a contingent happening or a symbolic device appreciated for its service to man's struggle to preserve, advance, and diversify the freedoms which his career as man start with. This career is an event in a world not made for it. It is a contingency, not a necessity, and it is a contingency working and fighting to establish itself as a necessity. The world of its labors and battles is itself a commingling of like endeavors of varying successes. Its arduous career develops in fact not as a pursuit of happiness but as a pursuit of liberty to which happiness attaches contingently. The cultures of mankind, its every civilization, are phases of this self-sustaining pursuit, sometimes attainments-in-passage, again passing regressions, but here or there, on the whole and in the long run, visions shaping action toward an economy of abundance in liberties.

The history of modernity has for its core a struggle between believers in a *philosophia perennis* and believers that change and chance are the springs of order, that chaos is not only the external but also internal environment of cosmos.

The former postulate the success of our struggle to keep on struggling upon some absolute rule and way, some revealed creed and prescribed code expressed in the institution of property and prescriptive law and order, and enforced by authoritarian policemen of the spirit and the flesh foreordained to this role, the topmost layer in a natural hierarchy of status and class. These believers are conservatives; for them "liberty" signifies this condition of man. The cultural economy they would support and guard is totalitarian. They figure in a strange fellowship of medievalizers, dixiecrats, tories, sacerdotalists, soi-disant nationalists, racists, fascists, nazis, communists, and communazis. One or another variety of them may be encountered anywhere. In China and Russia the self-named communist variety have formed an organization of power which has rendered these lands servile states, and have segregated men of science in a ghetto of their kind where they are compelled to exercise the freedoms essential to science to serve ends which, when applied to science, destroy it. Communist scientism is a major weapon in the perennial war of moral ideals which communist power wages against the free societies where change and chance are accepted as intrinsic to living-on; where status and class are treated as incidents of the free movement of equally free individuals, each of whom is different from every other, in their struggles to live on and progress; and all of whom more or less freely pool their efforts by means of property, institutions, all sorts of other associations, and "law and order" to attain these ends. In these societies authority is not an independent power imposing its rule from without; in these societies authority is power delegated, created by consensus, and assented to from within. Believers in such a world and such a society are liberals. They are pluralists and temporalists who hold that, on the record, science and its methods are the most satisfactory means (they are charged with "scientism" for this) which human enterprise has devised to prosper its survival and development—or to annul them.

This book is a study of the nature and role of liberty as experience, idea, and ideal, and of their bearings on the present phase of men's struggles to keep on struggling. A writing of it was practically completed some years ago, but was put aside to take up a related inquiry about the confrontation of men and their values in Israel, published recently under the title "Utopians at Bay."

I am all too aware that the speculations of physicists, astronomers, cosmologists, and mathematicians are just now diversifying with a speed and imaginative reach which would more than confirm Socates in his disillusion regarding their power to win to the ineluctable certainty he so craved. Nevertheless, I am presenting this study with almost no change from the first writing. However framed, the speculations advance the knowledge which is power over necessities, and such power liberates men from their non-human coercions, and harnesses those up to the service of human liberty. True, it neither dispenses with the ineffable nor postulates certainty. But it does far better than its competitors in dealing with the uncertainties man's spirit lives in and from. Become aware of its goal as its going, living is the meaning of liberty, liberty the intent of living; the uncertainties present all the "objective" certainty a mind can prehend and bet on. As William James wrote some generations ago: "Freedom ought to be freely espoused by men who can equally well turn their backs upon it. In other words, our first act of freedom, if we are free, ought to be in all inward propriety to affirm that we are free."

To Dr. Hadley Cantril, Senior Counsellor of the Institute of International Social Research at Princeton, and to Mrs. Dorothy Kuhn Oko, labor consultant at the New York Public Library, I am indebted for reading the manuscript and making helpful suggestions; to Mrs. Oko for her assistance with the index as well. To Dr. Alfred J. Marrow, of the Board of Trustees of the New School for Social Research, I am indebted for the interest which assured the publication of the essay. To these good friends and fellow-students of the problems of liberty, my cordial thanks.

HORACE M. KALLEN

The New School for Social Research
July, 1959.

1

Freedom as
the Human Condition

FREEDOM AS THE HUMAN CONDITION

1. Liberty as the Price of Security

Since, on the record, mankind everywhere crave to be at once safe and free, the human condition may be tantamount to an ongoing predicament. Certainly if any two single words betoken the dominant preoccupations of twentieth century civilization, the words are "security" and "liberty." Both carry many meanings, by no means independent. But a disposition persists to take them to stand for incompatible, even irreconcilable values, and in times of crisis the disposition becomes an attitude which would bar and beat down all others. Both in its chronic and acute phases, the predicament has made liberty and security alike occasions of laughter and of tears, and themes for comedy and tragedy, but liberty more so than security. As historians tell the tale, the ruling passion of civilized society, from 1776 through the second decade of the twentieth century, is better denoted by the word "liberty"; since the *crise plèthorique* of this century's third decade, society's dominant craving is better denoted by the word "security."

At that time the confident temper manifest with the turn of the century lapsed. The thrust toward adventure and libertarian change characterizing the world of ideas, the practices of the arts, the explorations of the sciences of nature and of man, the actualities of the relations between the sexes and between peoples, races and classes and occupations, was abruptly contained, even reversed. The aspiration of the First World War, "to make the world safe for democracy," was cut down into the plea "to make the world safe"; security became the key word. As the depression mounted, as the undertakings to meet and master its formations diversified and gathered momentum, and the idea, "security," led to programs of "social security," many enclaves of democratic society, American and transatlantic both, imagined social security as the sure effect of totalitarian organization and authoritarian rule alone. Russian Bolshevism, Italian Fascism, German Nazism gained open communications and secret missionaries, lay and clerical. And the latter were charged to undertake, in the name of social security, subversive aggression against the faith and works of the democratic establishments. In Spain, the newly formed republic was made the victim of all three of these totalitarianisms, whose Spanish likes, the Falange, produced the expression "Fifth Column," an expression now current in all societies. Free societies soon found the task of providing social security crossed and complicated with an added task of building national security, by resort to armament.

They found themselves first under the necessity of fighting a Second World War, perceived as a "war for survival," in order to stop aggression from abroad; and second, of directing the energies of the victors toward the formation of a global society wherewith the independent and sovereign states making themselves responsible for this society assure to one another peace and equal liberty, and to their peoples personal liberty and equal justice under law. The paragraphs of *The Four Freedoms* and the thirty articles of *The Universal Declaration of Human*

Rights propound this design. In them liberty receives again, though momentarily, precedence over security.

But even as momentary, the precedence is one rather of aspiration than achievement. While the free societies were demobilizing their fighting strength, their quondam totalitarian ally of the red left treacherously took over the rôle of the aggressor that had been played by the defeated brownshirts and blackshirts of the obscene right. The hot war waged by Nazis, Fascists, and Falangists was simply followed by the ongoing cold war, with hot spurts, waged by the Communists. The color, not the character, of the menace to democratic survival altered. Among free men aroused to that "early and provident fear" which Edmund Burke says "is the mother of safety," security very quickly regained its precedence over liberty. Concern for security became so wide and deep that poets and publicists took to calling their times "the age of anxiety"; theologians repristinated Calvin and Kierkegaard, in whom the resort to supernatural security was impelled by the anxieties of an agonized conscience; untheological metaphysicians projected existentialism, which appraises the pursuit of security as an anxiety-born illusion, equates human consciousness to anxiety as such, and declares anxiety itself to be the stuff of an existence without ground and without goal, a freedom all dread and horror, directed to death, and therefore blowing bubbles of salvation(the theologian's name for security) that can exist only so long as the blower blows.

Soon in the United States, legislative inquisitors, self-chosen vigilantes asserting a patriotic call, official policemen secret and open, and governmental loyalty boards pre-empted the foreground of public attention as defenders and vindicators of national security. Their creed and code came to be called "McCarthyism," and their ways were not slow in becoming those from which they said they were saving the country's faith and works. Having set themselves to catch the thieves of American safety, they found it most satisfactory to do so, in terms of the old saw, by themselves becoming the thieves of American freedom. Certain "intellectuals," who hatched the epithet "egghead" for others who differed from them, renewed the ancient sophism that neither a people or a person could be free and safe at the same time. The dogma that security and liberty are inveterate and irrevocable foes gained a new currency. Once more free men were warned that neither social nor national security can be congruent with personal liberty of any kind, whether of the body or the mind; that for national security, faith and reason must conform to an authoritarian creed, conduct to its co-ordinate code, and that both must obey a chain of command having power to impose the creed and enforce the code.

Of course, in this scheme, members of the hierarchy of administration could not themselves be subject to the rules nor bound to the creed they impose and the code they enforce. In relation to those, they are and functionally must needs be themselves free. Where they make up authoritarian structures within otherwise free societies—prisons are such, or military and sacerdotal establishments—they may be safe as well as thus free. The hierarchies of entirely totalitarian societies do not, however, regard themselves, and indeed may not be, safe; and accordingly they maintain for their own security a secret as well as a uniformed police, an inquisition, and censorship, whose duty it is everywhere to cultivate and to enhance into anxiety Edmund Burke's "early and provident fear" and to spy out and punish whoever is suspected of the improvidence of taking the liberty to deviate in any field in any way from creed or code. Among such security police, the tears of those who suffer, or witness, the practice of the inquisitional arts are welcome tokens of its success; laughter, on the other hand, is appraised as a liberty taken and hence as incurring the inescapable penalty.

These appraisals also have had their reverberations in free societies, and in the United States a candidate for the presidency was denounced because he treated certain issues raised by his opponents with laughter and not with tears.

2. Ages of Anxiety: Pre-Atomic and Post-Atomic

Since Hiroshima our age has come to be called the Atomic Age as well as Age of Anxiety. In many quarters, the West's spreading anxiety is held to be a consequence of the successful inquiries which led to the atomization of the atom, the invention of the fissionable atomic bomb and its more powerful fusionable epigon. The products of intra-atomic fission and inter-atomic fusion are explosions which set free an energy accounted to be as primally and ineffably consuming as that in the sun. The inventions are appraised as ominous for the survival, not of human civilization alone, but of all life on earth. Among the groups most plangent over this new, momentous, instant menace has been the company of physicists to whose invention the world owes the machinery which now threatens its survival—the machinery which breaks the bonds that hold the energies of earth in reciprocal arrest and liberates them into destruction. These men of science, feeling guilty of the pregnant threat to security, do not cease to urge the free creation of a global authority to police their inventions and to conform their employment to the upkeep, nourishment, and advance of the human enterprise everywhere.

But, regarding the import of their postulates for the human image of nature and for freedom as inward to nature, they say little. Yet breaking the bonds which bind energies into mass, and therewith transmuting mass into energy, does affect all our philosophies of freedom and necessity. Those men of science say even less regarding the import of these eventuations for the naked, elemental meaning of human liberty and human security or the conception of human destiny. Their anxiety did not ensue upon those momentous divergences from tradition; it ensued upon the contingency that tradition and innovation alike might mushroom up in the smoke of an atomic holocaust. They were weighed down, they continue to be weighed down, by a prescience of doom from which also the Kremlin hierarchy seems not exempt. Their foreboding was a new experience for men of science. Suddenly halted before the power they created, the physicists could not but look and listen and become afraid.

But the foreboding was no new experience for philosophical historians of the twentieth century. In the year 1900, Henry Adams, great-grandson of John and grandson of John Quincy Adams, had been a visitor to the World's Fair in Paris. In the Gallery of Machines he was brought to a standstill by the little device which was then the world's largest dynamo. Later, writing of this experience to a friend, he declared that "his historical neck was broken by the irruption of new forces." His specula-

tion on the impact of these forces led to his famous forecast that the middle of the century might witness the end
of everything. Already in 1901 he prophesied, in another
letter:

> All we can say is that, at the rate of increase of speed and
> momentum as calculated on the last fifty years, the present
> society may break its own damn neck in a definite but remote
> time, not exceeding fifty years. Either our society must stop
> or bust. I am rather inclined to think the situation is a new
> one. If anyone should tell me there is going to be hell to pay
> all around, I should not care to contradict him.
>
> You may think this is all nonsense but I tell you these
> are great times. Man has mounted science and is now run
> away with. Some day science may have mankind in its power,
> and the human race commit suicide by blowing up the world.

Most of what Adams wrote afterward became in one way
or another a "cosmic exploration" pursued in a succession
of arguments flowing from his foreboding, fleeing from
it, compensating for it, vindicating it.[1]

H. G. Wells, during the earlier decades of the century
a socialist interpreting the course of history as an ineluctable movement toward a democratic world-state,
became, in the later decades, an authoritarian appraiser of
the same course as a race between education and catas-
trophe. By 1946 he saw *Life at the End of its Tether*, and
argued in this, his last book, that "the end of everything
we call life is close at hand and cannot be evaded." Oswald
Spengler disclosed that the culture of the western world
was in decadence and foretold the debacle of modern
times in a divided mankind whose master-class cultivated
a global "caesarism" punctuated by palace intrigues, while

---

1. This is the impelling motivation of *The Virgin and the Dynamo*, the
Letter to Teachers of History, *Mont Saint Michel and Chartres*, and the
widely read *Education of Henry Adams*.

its subject multitudes continued in the cycles of an animal existence made up of "zoological occurrences." In *Jahre der Entscheidung* he prophesied the irruption into Europe of a white-led colored proletariat marching from Africa. Arnold Toynbee writes more theologically but with hardly more cheerfulness; Aldous Huxley—before his conversion to an esoteric optimism—, George Orwell, and any number of current projectors of an image of the future via "science-fiction" express the same essential feeling of doom as Spengler and Adams. *Brave New World, Animal Farm, 1984, Fahrenheit #61,* and the like are, of course, allegories, not histories. But their valuations are consonant with those of the historians. To all, the future of mankind, if any, is a future without freedom; and to many, without security either. The most hopeful image of man that they might project is the figure drawn by W. H. Auden, whose verses first signalized the present age as "the age of anxiety." This figure is a projection of statistical anonymity, a distressed appraisal of the citizen kept safe and sound by a democratic state at mid-century.

THE UNKNOWN CITIZEN

(To IS/07/M/378
This Marble Monument Is Erected by the State)

> He was found by the Bureau of
>   Statistics to be
> One against whom there was no
>   official complaint
> And all the reports of his conduct
>   agree
> That, in the modern sense of an
>   old-fashioned word, he was a saint.
> For in everything he did he served
>   the Greater Community.

Except for the War till the day
    he retired
He worked in a factory and never
    got fired.
But satisfied his employers,
    Fudge Motors, Inc.
Yet, he wasn't a scab or odd in
    his views.
For his Union reports that he paid
    his dues.
(Our report on his Union shows
    it was sound)
And our Social Psychology workers
    found
That he was popular with his mates
    and liked a drink.
The Press are convinced that he
    bought a paper every day
And that his reactions to advertisements
    were normal in every way.
Policies taken out in his name prove
    that he was fully insured.
And his Health-card shows he was
    once in a hospital but left it cured.
Both Producers Research and
    High-Grade living declare
He was fully sensible to the
    advantage of the installment plan
And had everything necessary to
    the Modern Man.
A phonograph, a radio, a car and
    a Frigidaire.
Our researches into Public Opinion
    are content
That he held the proper opinions for
    the time of year;
When there was peace, he was for
    peace; when there was war, he went.
He was married and added five

children to the population.
Which our Eugenist says was the
    right number for a parent
    of his generation.
And our teachers report that he
    never interfered with their
    education.
Was he free: Was he happy?
    The question is absurd:
Had anything been wrong, we
    should certainly have heard.

The satire needs no comment at this time. But implicit in the verse-man's "absurd" question there is, as no reader can fail to recognize, an idea that security must be incompatible not only with liberty but likewise with happiness. It suggests that the only security which can be compatible is such as would be a means to liberty and nothing else. It suggests that liberty comes first, that it is intrinsic to the original nature of man, and that the social exaltation of collective security and degradation of personal liberty is the perversion of a servant into a master, the worship of a fetish and idolization of a tool.

3. The Import of the New Physics for Liberty, Human and Non-Human

The newer sciences of nature, alike in themselves and in their extension to human nature, bring strengthening to such suggestions, which are themselves transpositions of older perceptions of *genus humanum*, perceptions whereon is postulated the democratic revolution going on among the peoples of the globe. These older seeings— alike the pluralistic, as by Thomas Hobbes, and the monistic, as by Baruch Spinoza—generalized the generalizations of Galileo concerning the patterns of movements and events on the earth, in the heavens, and in the tools and works of man. Those philosophies set forth what has come to be known as "the mechanical view of nature." In this view, nature's generic model is the clock. Every clock is a machine. Every clock consists of moving parts every one of which pushes or pulls some other from rest into motion or from one motion into a different motion, while the whole that the parts add up to is itself motionless. The sequence of give and take from part to part can be stated in precise and unchanging equations which are the laws of the motion of these parts and the whole's disclosure of its own immobility. The more precisely their motions are delimited and the more consequentially their relations are established, the more correctly the clock is understood as a dynamic system. The procedures render the idea of the clock "clear and distinct." They render the equations which present it so "adequate" to its inner sequences that they constitute the "truth" of the system—the truth for those who believed the whole to be a secondary formation subsisting as the eternal configuration of eternal parts or atoms, coming together or separating in an empty, unbounded space; and the truth for those who believed the whole to be one eternal, total substance, and its every part or atom a self-diversification so related to all the others that without them it can neither be, nor be clearly, distinctly, and adequately thought. The former were, and still are, pluralists. The latter were, and still are, monists.

Pluralists and monists both used the word *nature* to denote the dynamic system. Both conceived the truth of it as a Euclidean pattern of forces arranged in orders following from their amounts. Both believed that the amounts were combinations repeating identical minima always and everywhere the same. Both distinguished the sequences of combination, making up the orders as configurations of cause and effect. Both imagined the entirety of the sequences as a One sustaining these distinctions without difference. Spinoza signalized this One as at once *Natura Naturans*, nature the producer, and *Natura Naturata*, nature the product. It was Spinoza alone, however, who used the word *nature* interchangeably with the word *God: "Deus sive Natura."*

For the great number who did not so use it, but acquiesced in the idea of nature whence the usage derived, *God* meant exclusively *naturans, nature* meant exclusively *naturata.* But they believed also that the inalterable laws of nature were the laws of "nature's God" and that the equation of their variables revealed Deity as Eternal Reason and disclosed the ultimacy of a providence the same always and everywhere. Hobbes used the equation in his *Leviathan* to ground an authoritarian social order whose preponderant force alone keeps mankind from falling back into the terrified, solitary, poor, nasty, brutish anarchy of his primal war of all against all. Spinoza, in the *Political Tractate*, and indeed in all his other expressions, used the equation to ground an ideal of equality in right which one hundred years later became one of the articles of faith underlying the Democratic Revolution: "Everything in nature," Spinoza reasoned, "has as much right through nature as it has power to exist and work. . . . Whatever any man does by the rule of his own nature, that he does by a perfect natural right, and has right over nature so far as by his power he preserves his own being." And inasmuch as right is self-preserving power, and power is right of self-preservation, but only as items of nature's products, and inasmuch as the entirety of nature as ongoing production comes equally to a focus in each of them, all men are equal in right.

As Spinoza here uses the word *nature*, he intends by it the teeming diversity of all that becomes, goes on, and ceases—including the many alternative meanings of nature which differing philosophers select from the unceasingly diversifying aggregate—seen under "the aspect of eternity." But the selections are not made "under the aspect of eternity." The meaning chosen signalizes the right of some singular power struggling to preserve itself. The choice of it is invidious and made in order to rationalize or justify the chooser's preferential weighting of some intention, desire, or object that he cherishes and fights for, against alternative preferences of other choosers, reciprocally embattled. Each declares the others' meaning of nature *un*natural because they are opposed. Yet on the record, there is no human experience—be it of men and their relations or of the nature of things—which is not signalized as "natural" in some connections and as "unnatural" in others. In these signalizings, nature is also the common name for the diversity of irreconcilable conflicting preferences felt to have no sanction in themsalves, nor any inward authenticity. They are therefore supplied therewith by means of rationalizations equally irrational, in the darkling faith that rationality is born of a union of irrationals. Theology has many instances of such natures, constructed in order to rationalize the claims of sacerdotal power-structures or of rebels against such structures. Spinoza's "nature" comprehends those, together with their rivals and alternatives, and purports to account for them all.

The nature bespoken by Jefferson and other spokesmen of the Democratic Revolution varied from Spinoza's
in that it postulated deism and not pantheism. All the
same, its import for human nature and human relations
was that of Spinoza's. In the view of these witnesses,
equality of right is the end to which security is a means
and only a means. The signers of the American Declaration of Independence bet their all on the profession of
faith that all men are created equal, that they are endowed with certain inalienable rights, and that governments are instituted "to secure these rights," especially
"life, liberty, and the pursuit of happiness." The latter are
the notably innate ones, the stuff of human nature, the
immanent ends of human existence, at once its process,
naturans, and its product, *naturata*. Where they do not
secure themselves, that which does secure them is a secondary, a derivative, construction, nothing else than a
means to themselves as ends. The means may, and on
occasion does, the Declaration emphasizes, usurp the
ends, subverts and betrays that which it was instituted to
secure.

In sum: When human nature is set in the perspectives
of "the mechanical view of nature," as the Democratic
Revolution set it, human nature is understood as *ab
origine* a configuration of natural forces or powers whose
equivalents in social discourse are "unalienable rights."
The persistence and development of this configuration
have no guarantees. They are a hazard, not a security.
The configuration's existence is a struggle to go on struggling which, without liberty, could not even begin to be.
Life and the pursuit of happiness are thus postulated on
liberty; and liberty is but a univocal sign for a multitude
of diverse liberties, among which those that the Bill of

Rights of the American Constitution names are appraised as critically significant. But all, the least no less than the most important, designate personal experience of alternatives, processes of deliberation consummating in personal choices and decisions. And of all, the first and last freedom, the matrix of every other and the vital urge in their growth and fruitage, is the freedom of the mind: "I have sworn," said Jefferson, "upon the altar of God, eternal hostility against every form of tyranny over the mind of man," and he dedicated the university which he founded to "the illimitable freedom of the human mind to explore and expose every subject susceptible of its contemplation." Regarding what follows the loss of this freedom, hear Judge Learned Hand, more than a century and a quarter later: ". . . As soon as we cease to pry at random, we shall come to rely upon accredited bodies of authoritative dogma; and as soon as we come to rely upon accredited bodies of authoritative dogma, not only are the days of our liberty over, but we have lost the password that has hitherto opened to us the gates of success as well."

4. How Liberty Became an Unalienable Right

Among those who appraised as self-contradiction the grounding of human liberty in a nature all mechanical necessity, proponents of authoritarian doctrines and disciplines had libertarian allies. The latter also opined that "the mechanical view of nature" was more consonant with Hobbes' authoritarian *Leviathan* or Rousseau's irrevocable *General Will*. Nevertheless, from Galileo's times to Einstein's, the wave of the future appears to have been a swirl of aspiration postulating impartially both liberation from human tyranny and attainment of human security on infallible workings of "the laws of nature and of nature's God." Or, if the postulants laid their bets on the laws of nature alone, they still endowed them with a providence which would guide the course of human events to the wished-for, and hence foregone, conclusion.

Among the gamblers on undirected nature, some few constructed their tips from the findings of Darwin, others from the speculations and dogmas of Marx; both served to promote a human hazard into a cosmic guarantee, both purported to close forever the open issue of the questing passion's final consummation. Not many would see that if the freedoms are real, no closure can be final, no consummation can be forever; if the freedoms are real, the best any human enterprise can lastingly achieve is some compromise, some orchestration with others formed by the free participation of each in the choices of the others. To quote Learned Hand again, from what he recently told the Board of Regents of the University of the State of New York:

> Most of the issues that mankind sets out to settle it never does settle; the dispute fades into the past unsolved, though perhaps it may be renewed as history and fought over again. It disappears because it is replaced by some compromise that, though not wholly satisfactory to either side, offers a tolerable substitute for victory; and he who would find the substitute needs an endowment as rich as possible in experience, an experience which makes the heart generous, and provides his mind with an understanding of the hearts of others.

Such compromises are organizations of liberty. They are innovations establishing a reciprocal security created by all of the parties to the compromise in order to assure to each and for each his independence and freedom.

5. Chance and Liberty

During the half-century past, the physical sciences have produced alternatives to "the mechanical view of nature" which are held to do its job of accounting for events better. Concurrently, several philosophising physicists have come to opine that the inconsistency between natural necessity and human freedom has been dissipated. One word for the alternatives thus metaphysically appraised is "relativity." Another is "field theory." A third is "quantum mechanics." The ideas are held to supplement the temporalism of the evolutionary hypothesis, but are not regarded as themselves necessarily self-consistent or consistent with one another. By and large, however, controlled experiments provide support for the speculative perception that analysis—whether cyclotronic, bevatronic, mathematical, or semantic—is stopped at a surgent spontaneity which can be referred to no ground, must be taken for its own ground, and could as well not happen as happen. Traditional words for such spontaneity are *chance, contingency, freedom,* and the like. The traditional view of the experiences which these words name has been, among scientists and philosophers, consummatory. They are appraised as illusions or fallacies or both—this with due regard to their persistence in commonsense and their powerful and honorific role in the cultures of mankind. Many of the cultures translate the experiences into miracles worked by Providence, or worship chance and fortune as divinities; others humanize them as Lady Luck, and all of them cultivate games of chance satisfying the gambler's spirit. This spirit, which signalizes every sort and condition of *genus humanum,* nourishes vitality on uncertainty, existence on struggle, and cannot be at rest with infallible security. It refuses to make its wager with destiny, however it defines the stakes, a bet on a sure thing.

Now the new, non-mechanical views of nature do not condemn chance, contingency, and freedom as illusions. Some who speak for the new views even admit them as ineffables of experience or as postulates providing the groundless and ungroundable grounds of their systems of nature.

The nature projected by such systems is not, however, a *natura naturans* altogether without law and necessary connection. On the contrary, it lives and works in both. But the very knowledge of nature, which acquaintance with them enables, demotes the systems from the eternity and universality that had hitherto been their attributes. They are no longer taken as uncaused or self-caused causes, but as consequences which have become causes. Origins and histories are assigned to them, and the origins are the ineffable chance comings. The surgent spontaneities and contingencies had been ruled out of nature as illusions of man's consciousness and occasionally located outside of nature in a supernatural creator who had created once, and then never again, even though the *never* had to be tempered by the miraculous divine interpositions which salvation from some crisis required. But astronomical churchmen such as Canon Lemaitre transpose this notion into the terms of modern astrophysics by the image of one primal total atom exploding, and producing in a stretch of time not longer than fifteen clock-minutes, all the elements of the existing universe and the laws of their combination and separation, while George Gamow has devised a non-clerical projection of this image.

The basic distinction between the clerical and the non-clerical comes in the signification of *law*. For the churchman and theologian it signalizes commandment; "the laws of nature and of nature's God," however proximately accounted for, are ultimately orders issued by authority and obeyed by the subject of authority. In effect the laws are statutes and even if disobeying them is impossible to nature, it is possible to man, if not in Thomistic reality, then in Calvinistic appearance. For the unchurchly scientist, on the other hand, *law* signifies simply the operative invariant relations between events, generating predictable variations by the repetition of identicals. Scientist and theologian both, however, postulate one sole changeless source of change, a ground always and everywhere the same, which the theologian dramatizes into Eternal God and the scientist envisions as Universal Nature.

But in recent years theoretical physicists have devised pluralistic and altering singular alternatives to these sole material or psychological identities. Such non-mechanical views of original nature as those expounded by Hoyle, Bondi, or Gold, signalize spontaneity as nature's uttermost inwardness; they postulate that which "she" is as ongoing bursts of creation *ex nihilo*, as successive becomings flowing together and linking up. They appraise nature's laws and the necessary connections they denote, as developmental formations eventuating from the interplay of the diverse spontaneities and ever undergoing modification by them. Nature, in this conspectus, is ongoing process, origination and becoming; her laws are—as Charles Peirce once argued and William James agreed—habits acquired, not eternal relations; her forms and varieties are contingent formations, not universal patterns, and their structure, occurrence, and distribution are statistical events, not inevitable sequences. In this conspectus of nature, force and form, figure and function, power and pattern, are so interpenetrated that the metaphysician's distinction between *Natura Naturans* and *Natura Naturata* becomes an error of judgment, shown up by its consequences. The ancient undying analogy between nature and the virgin motherhood of the female of the species regains its meaningfulness, and the usage which signalizes the total conceivable course of events as "Mother Nature's" parthenogenesis recovers a propriety made indecent by "the mechanical view." For nature now names the process of infinite and indeterminate (the two words may denote a distinction without a difference) fertility at the aggregate heart of things; it is the word for ongoing processes of initiation and nativity and development and change which render existence, eventuation, and being the configurative tension of the encounter and reciprocal arrest of diverse becomings. Essence, form, idea, potentiality, eternity might then be recognized as being's other names, every one of them standing for a limit or boundary which the central propulsions are unceasingly pressing to penetrate and soon or late do.

If man is indigenous to such a nature, biography is no illusion and history no mirage, even when their perspectives are arbitrary and their intent and organization are special pleas. In this nature, man is authentically the natural man with his inborn natural rights. In this nature, the dynamic of every human life is what the liver experiences it as, from his genes on—a struggle to go on struggling; every individual's personality is an ongoing unique formation of self-orchestrating habits of perceiving and venturing which his biography uniquely spans.

As a natural of such a nature, liberty would be integral to man's nativity and to the formation of his singularity as this man and no other.

6. "Field Theory," Mobility, and the Indeterminate

There is a trend in the sciences of body and mind which feeds the belief that this is the case.

But the comfortable certainty of the "mechanical view" is not easily abandoned, even by the inventors and perfectors of non-mechanical views of nature. Theoretical physicists like Einstein or Schrödinger continue to cultivate the determinism upon which the results of their own inquiries cast doubt. They could hardly approve octogenarian Bertrand Russell's confession that his lifelong quest for certainty consummates in the conclusion that the only certainty is uncertainty—a sober transposition of the favorite verbal paradox among sophists of the absolute, the eternal, and the universal, that change alone does not change. And the disposition continues formidable and vigorous among the great majority of men of science in all fields (from nuclear physics and astronomy to human physiology and psychology) either to discount the trends toward the repristination of spontaneity in nature and human nature or to reinterpret the findings in necessitarian terms. The belief prevails that science cannot be science without determinism; that with determinism it provides a knowledge of the courses of events, human and non-human, vastly more reliable and efficacious than any other discipline of the mind, vastly more trustworthy in forecasting the future, understanding the past, and controlling the present.

Nevertheless, the reliability is not rendered absolute, nor the efficacy brought to maximal precision until the instrument of measurement itself becomes a part of whatever it measures. But by becoming thus inward to its object, the instrument changes the object and so defeats the ends to which it is the means. For, to serve these ends, the object must continue unaltered and relations between it and the measuring tool external. The more microscopic and particularized a research, the more delicate and precise its instruments of determination, the more likely is delicacy to consummate in uncertainty, precision in indeterminancy, efficacy in ambiguity. The scientific disclosure, begun with a knower's propositions, ends up as a believer's postulate. Soon or late we reach today's intra-atomic version of antiquity's eleatic paradox—the Zenonian demonstrations that a flying arrow is at rest—transposed into Heisenberg's "principle of indeterminancy."

For Heisenberg's explorations came out with the conclusion that particles in motion have no position, particles at a position have no momentum. A position is a frontier, motion is an alteration of frontier dissipating it within the particle as well as beyond, by spanning "beyond." Hence, no exclusive identification of any particle can be made. As the best-known scientific sacrifice to the Federal Government's anxiety-driven pursuit of security, the nuclear physicist, J. Robert Oppenheimer, notes, in his *Science and the Common Understanding*, "If we ask whether the position of the electron remains the same, we must say 'no'; if we ask whether the electron's position changes with time, we must say 'no'; if we ask whether the electron is at rest, we must say 'no'; if we ask whether it is in motion, we must say 'no.'"

To think the particle significantly is, it would appear, to give it identity as an ongoing identification of multitudinous successive differings into a confluent same; that is, to think it an event, a drop, a process like a life of birth, maturation, senescence, and death; a quantum so confluent with other quanta as together to shape up atoms and molecules and aggregations and configurations of molecules of various dimensions (some composed by hundreds of thousands of atoms), all mobile and moving, both as composed wholes and in their composing parts.

Such mobility is ineffable. It can have no parallel representation. Certainly representations are devised. But all are perforce perceptible, comparatively microscopic "models," no more like the unperceived confluences they signify than shorthand characters are like the changing actualities they are intended to be signs of. Arrangements such as Bohr's, of electrons, protons, and the like, Euclidean or not, can figure only as denotable forms, only as configurations, whereas the confluences they signalize are more reliably designated "fields," with each field evincing an inward indeterminancy singular to itself. "Field theory" is today a working hypothesis of many of the sciences of man, from individual psychology to cultural anthropology. Their practitioners are, on the whole, less concerned to establish necessary connection and more to delineate statistical distributions. And all are more or less aware that the ways and values of no individual contributor to the distribution-pattern—even as of no single electron in an atom—can by its means be identified or his personal history foretold.

For this distribution-pattern is what necessary connection looks like, close to. If the repetition of identicals and the identity of indiscernibles which necessary connection postulates were discoverable, the sciences, including mathematics, would be in fact the comfortable hypo-thetico-deductive systems which they seek to become in symbol. But mathematicians more than all must postulate ineffables, incalculables, indemonstrables, if they are to demonstrate, calculate, or prove at all. Without such they could devise neither equations nor any other technique of relating wherewith they purport to solve mathematical problems. But no ineffable observably repeats and only repeats. There can be no statistic of precisely the same. Diversity is assumed or somehow slips in. And without indeterminancy, how could it? As, more than a genera-tion ago, Nils Bohr suggested, if a physiologist were able so to understand all of a man's somatic and intrasomatic behaviors that he could predict them infallibly at any and all moments of the man's existence, he would be able to do so only in virtue of his command of the physics, the chemistry, the pathology, and all the other aspects of his subject's *intra* and *inter-cellular* struggle for existence. But to acquire this command, our physiologist would have to pass from apparently detached observation to participating manipulation; and such manipulation would so alter the observer's original subject that his eventual findings would apply to quite a different subject, a sub-ject made different by the process of inquiry itself.

The point of this illustration is that an inquirer or observer does not, and cannot in fact, long remain outside the system he inquires into. The more closely he looks, the deeper in he gets. An observer looking at a city from an airplane is above and beyond it and apparently able to make a ground plan of its skylines without interacting with them. On the ground, he is in direct contact with the forms and forces upon and within it—bumping, stopping and being stopped, pushing through, going round or under or over, and thereby changing the shape of things whose unchanged shape he purposes to identify. The farther in he gets, the more diversifying his role. He either becomes a force within the system, changing its inward pattern, or it becomes a force which alters him, or both. Mostly, it is both. The transactions between him and the city diversify and complicate. Begun as the somewhat one-sided simplicities of looking and seeing, they consummate in the dynamic reciprocities orchestrating a symbiotic existence.

He himself, the party of the first part in these transactions, entering upon them from some instant present, enters them as a present whose identity is his living past; that is, an ongoing formation of a personality whose beginnings could be formally dated from his conception by his parents and his eventuation be followed through the transactions of birth and growth up to the moment of his inquiry. His presence would here span his personality as it makes itself via the transactions between his heredity as impatterned and particularized in his genes and his successive environments—starting with his mother's womb, and moving in and through all the subsequent surroundings of persons, places, thoughts, and things and their compounding relations. Conventional names for these compoundings are "family," "school," "church," "club," "gang," "job," "party," "country" and the like. "He," "him," "individual," "person," are at long last signs or symbols of the unique line of development initiated in his genes and altering direction and character with the unceasing give-and-take between him and his endlessly diversifying surroundings.

His struggle to go on struggling and to grow as man

consists of this give-and-take. It may be viewed as a chronological sequence checked off on a calendar day after day, year after year, birthday after birthday. So viewed, his existence spans the successive constellations of starts and stops, of goings and goals, which together make up the trajectory of the years of his life. They follow one another like the instant and separate stills of a motion-picture film, or the items of a statistician's curve, or the photon of a physicist's wave. But the same events may be, and are, far more commonly viewed as a total, immediate reality; as a living, thinking individuality, present here and now. This view looks upon the physical mass of a man of flesh and bone, consciously talking, standing, sitting, walking, running, pausing, laughing, weeping, performing all the acts that knowledge and know-how can perfect or devise. This view envisions an integral person; his somatic constitution and diathesis; his ruling passions, his philosophic stance—his entire life-space as his ways of thinking, feeding, working, loving, hating, fighting, playing, weeping, and laughing changefully delineate it; and as their inward harmonies and discords unify, compact, and bound, into the singularity of his visible presence and determinate character, the successive experiences of his personal history.

A common analogue for this ongoing personal history is the concentrated, tridimensional action-image on the motion-picture screen. A less common one is the nuclear physicist's "particle" as compacted "wave," or his "energy" as bound up into "mass." Perhaps the singular configurational symbol which the statistician creates by ordering the data of his study into a distribution-curve is also an analogy.

Physiology, biology, and other sciences of living

bodies, mammalian or whatever, are operations on such personal histories. The sciences purport to disclose the body's form by separating organ from organ, cell from cell, process from process; by distinguishing present structure and function, and by imputing a past history only if adequate explanation seems to require it, although the total presence is of past history all compact. Few sciences stay taxonomic only; the most static and classifying predicates sequences of change, whether developmental or deteriorative. All tend to treat biological individuals as dynamic systems, ultimately as a teamplay of reciprocally interacting heart and lungs and kidneys and liver and digestive tract, glands of internal secretion and muscles, brain and nervous system (with its peripheral and sympathetic segments, its end-organs of internal perception in joints and muscles, and of external perception at the skin and in the eyes and ears and mouth and nose); all are laved by Claude Bernard's kidney-regulated "internal environment"—that interstitial plasma which the bloodstream carries as it cleans and feeds and defends these organs, and which is a first condition of their living and thriving together as a psychosomatic system.

Moreover, the system, and each of its organs, is conceived to be an evolutionary formation composed of single but not identical cells. Each cell is in its turn a biochemical configuration of molecules making up the many varieties of living stuffs—protoplasm, proteins, fats, down to the last singular diversification analyzed out in some biological laboratory. Farther analysis separates the molecules into component atoms, and the atoms, by whatever agencies of divorce and segregation, into the electrons, protons, neutrons, and other particle-waves with their indeterminacies, which are today's "ultimates" of reality.

Indeterminancy is a potential inward to every cell of every organ and an actuality of the whole organism's struggle to preserve its wholeness, a wholeness which alters as it is preserved and continues only as it changes.

7. Evolution, "Field Theory," and the Idea of Personality

A current term for this ongoing process of altering repetition is homeostasis. At any one phase the swerves from identity—for which Darwin's "spontaneous variations" might still be an apt expression—are imperceptibly minute, and may take diversely measurable times to compound into perceptibility. Unless this were so, differentiation might be the same as total abolition of identity, and not an evolution; for evolution consists of a very slow succession of quanta of variations, compenetrating and accumulating as they succeed one another. Unless this were so, process would consist only in sheer chance and destruction and not in ongoing change creating new orders of connection as well. Evolution eventuates in a self-orchestration of chances; it is the inward process by which a same diverges from its own sameness, when the alteration is neither implicit nor predictable and might more rightly be appraised an emergency and not an emergent.

True evolution, hence, is not emergent evolution, whether Morgan's kind or Bergson's or any other. Aficionados of an emergent evolution postulate, knowingly or unknowingly, necessary connection; their *terminus ad quem* is somehow or other a foregone conclusion from their *terminus a quo*. The process excludes chance. True evolution postulates only free variations, chance comings and goings that modify but do not demolish sameness. They may modify by adding, subtracting, or both. Once they have occurred, the "natural selection" which signifies success or failure in "the struggle for survival" repeats the ongoing process of change within the whole as batteries of exchanges between the whole and its environment. The aggregation of surroundings, whatever their formations, are no less modifiable and modified by chances and changes than the organisms they environ. They are not at all rigid inalterables to which the altering organism must conform.

"Fit" is a qualification of environment as well as of organism. The "fitting" of the two is reciprocal. It is not a conformation but a transaction wherein the most elementary organism so orders the environment to its survival as to retain its singularity of difference.

The *species humanum* does this more radically; it refuses to stay fit for any original nature that environs it, but deals with that nature in such wise as to render it fitter for its human singularities, humanizing it almost entirely. We call these transactions of mankind with nature, culture, civilization. They stretch from the cultivation of the earth and whatever lives thereon, to the creation of elements, such as plutonium and its successors not produced by nature at all. Together, all the works of man compound into an external environment analogous to the individual organism's internal environment. As folkways, customs, and mores they envelop, they nourish, they regulate, and they protect the humanity of human beings. But unlike the internal environment, they are far from keeping always and everywhere the same, or nearly the same. None is a necessary condition, a predestined consequence or a foregone conclusion certain to

follow from the primal initiatives of *Natura Naturans*.
"The laws of nature and of nature's God" have no such
demonstrable certainty. Certainty here is a posture of the
will-to-believe, not a disclosure of rational enquiry. If the
laws are what they are said to be, they imply all events
equally, none preferentially; the opposite of any event
is no less necessary than the event itself; and where all
occurrences are equally bound to happen, the fact that
one does and others do not can be accounted for only by
postulating a particular freedom and contingency in the
sources of nature whence the concrete singularities of
existence spring.

So with cultures, so with civilizations, so with the
human individuals and the associations of them whose
external environments they become. Every one of them,
like every individual and every individual cell of the
individual person, has at its core a potential of indeterminancy which all genuine novelties and originations of
a culture at last attest. Being variations and innovations,
hence unbalancing forces or influences, their lot is that of
Darwin's spontaneities in the origin of species. The
societies they occur in are apt to fear, not favor them.
Their struggle for survival is apt to be a conscious struggle
to escape "acculturation" *of* themselves and to effect
"acculturation" *to* themselves. They may be denounced
as corrupters of society, spreaders of evil, and treated with
laughter or tears. They may be approved as strength-
bringers, as nourishers and prophets of progress. Neither
appraisal need derive from the matter or the manner of
their being, either must largely follow from what the
appraiser believes is its impact on his value-system and
his personal fortunes. The appraisal is intrinsic to the
transactions wherein he deals with them, and signalizes

his belief that the deal he gets, as against the deal he gives, is "new," "square," "fair," "lucky," "unlucky," or "raw."

8. The Conscious Self as Value-System

The word "appraisal" points to a component of transactions that most are believed to be without. Convention imputes it to living organisms and commonly to the *species humanum* alone. The component is awareness or consciousness. That which lacks it is "matter," that is, the blind, unselecting, unselected, undistinguished, undistinguishing flux of events, the indifferent becoming which has no first and no last, no better or worse, right or wrong, beautiful or ugly, comic or tragic, nor any commandment or any duty. Consciousness installs all these. Its supervention initiates a center of preference and selection, a self-referent singularity whose existence brings into concurrent existence meanings of which the consciousness is the seat and dynamic sustenance, and of which the environs, however near or far, are always content and often consequence. Convention's word for these meanings is "value."

The word "value" signalizes numberless attitudes toward eventuations of experience. They range from those various acceptances of the diverse and their identification with or compenetration into "self," which are commonly called "liking" and "love," to the manifold repulsions and alienations for which the common words are "dislike" and "hate." On occasion one or another individual reaches an articulation of awareness that discriminates the attitudes which compenetrate into his sense of selfhood and thus make up the ineffable feel of his singularity and worth. To discern, recall, and hold these discriminations his means are language and other signs and symbols; and his power to produce, diversify, and use those is indeed among the most notable differentiae of his nature as man. They are the instruments wherewith he arranges a symbolic abstract configuration of his selfhood to form a sequential distribution of attractions and repulsions, of preferences and rejections. Usage signalizes the objects of these conscious postures as goods and evils, virtues and vices, validities, valors, and their negations.

9. The Mind, Its Functions, and the Value-System

The configurations into which the distributions come are the individual's value-system. To be more than merely a fantasy in words and images, more than merely a system of tokens betokening one another, the system's meanings must needs both span the person's past and project his future, insofar as his future is a projectable program of action and not simply a desirable prophecy. This is to say that his instant presence, the solid, ongoing psycho-somatic particular figure that an onlooker perceives here and now, must needs be diversified into the successive eventuations which compose his past and the succeeding pretensions which he desires and intends for his future. Such diversifications and desirings are usually called recollection, reflection, and will, and postulated on "faculties" of memory, of anticipation, and of deliberation. Their synergy consummates in a passing closure called decision. Actively or passively, the consummation engages the whole man, both as a standing present event and as an ongoing personal history. The engagement is his struggle to go on struggling whereof his altering survival constitutes itself. Its existence is at once process and product, a becoming whose frontiers his value-system informs and maps.

In the nature of the case, to be human is to devise, or to accept and alter, and to live by, some such system. Every individual, in whatever culture, achieves a system of values somehow singular to himself, with its own singularity of clearness and distinctness. Very largely, to exist means for him to endeavor to maintain the mapped articulation of his values, to inhibit their mutation within, and to extend their prevalence and defend them against penetration or permeation by other men's different values from outside. His endeavor expresses itself in the transactions with friends and foes which the religious cults institutionalize as rite and rote, while the "normative sciences" of the philosophic schools purport to disclose and encode them. The latter are the reasonings and the rationalizations which claim for infallible conclusion the vision and ownership of *the* Good, *the* Right, *the* True, *the* Beautiful and *the* Divine.

So far as anybody knows, none of this happens where there is no body and no brain; indeed, where there are no human body, brain, and nervous system, in all their multitudinous complexity and elaboration. The explorations of psychoneurologists, neurophysiologists, and surgeons have brought together a large corpus of information concerning brain and nerves. This discloses them as by and large an electrodynamic system of cell-structures in sustained transactions with one another and with the body's muscles, glands, and bones and other components. The transactions are at once individual and collective. They serve the inquirers as points of departure for inferences regarding their import for the processes of feeling, perceiving, remembering, intending, imagining, conceiving, reasoning, and the other specifications of psychic happening which may or may not be in his awareness.

In the light of the assembled observations and inferences, consciousness would be signalized as an activity that so relates its field of operations to the intra-organic events, of which the psychosomatic aspects of the self is the ongoing consummation, as to keep it a dynamic configuration of confluent action-sequences. Selfhood thus may be described as a pulsing "field" whose focus is the body and whose fringed frontier is ever in process of being enlarged, diminished, reshaped. But always, where the body is, I am; where the body is, is *here*; what participates instrumentally in the body's transactions, is *me*; that with which the transactions are entered into is *you*, or *this-there* (be it thing or thought). Where the body is, is *subject, here*; where not, *object, there*. Awareness, hence, looks like an engagement at a frontier indeterminately between here and there, *I* and *me, I* and *you, I* and *that*. The incandescence of a searchlight illuminating whatever stirs beyond the self's boundary has been invoked as an analogue for it; so has a mirror giving back with a difference his own image to one who looks therein. But these are static parallels for an altering process. In any individual's experience of being conscious, in any person's self-consciousness, consciousness is a frontier-pioneer watchful of *there, that, you,* and *they*; it is either initiating their intake and assimilation, via a multitude of formations, into *here, me,* and *I* and *we*, or setting afoot their evasion, extrusion, ex-communication, and interdict.

The initiation of either the adient or the abient transaction appears to be an act of perception. The initiating agencies appear to be the senses—touch, temperature, taste, smell, hearing, seeing, with their advances and retreats. Those two words denote ideo-motor muscle-sense—the feeling likely ever to compenetrate all others because it is the consummatory dynamic in every formation of consciousness.

10. Does Consciousness Exist?: Or Consciousness and the Brain Electric

For this feeling is awareness as of a passage passing. Being the experience of experience, or awareness of awareness, it is ineffable. Analysis cannot separate it into components nor synthesis reconstruct it from them. The closest study of mind and body, of their composition and behaviors, uses the consciousness it would discern in the unsuccessful endeavors to discern it. But it is self-evident and nothing else evidences it. What it discloses is so far neither consciousness "as such" nor any of its complications. All that investigation turns up is the diversity of occasions when consciousness supervenes or snuffs out. Long ago William James raised the question, *Does consciousness exist?* and certain schools of psychology, such as the behaviorist, deny that consciousness is anything at all. Other schools have intermittently denoted that which supervenes as "mind-stuff," "the subliminal," "the subconscious," "the unconscious." Since the invention of psychoanalysis, the last term, "the unconscious," has come to pervade usage. All the terms appear to have been devised in order to suggest a difference from consciousness which is not substantive but relational, and which the term "experience" includes. Thus, the psychoanalysts' "unconscious" is psychic energy *in potentia*, mind-stuff asleep yet astrain as a wound-up spring is astrain, while consciousness is the spring in release, mind-stuff awake. Although the Freudian mechanics of mind move out from the body-parts and propensities and describe an orbit around them, psychoanalytical logic employs the organism and its organs as locations, as markers, or as instruments, not as forces; psychoanalytic systems, of whatever denomination, at once postulate and disregard them. The determinist dynamic of *id*, *ego*, *superego*, with their erotisms and other action-gradients, calls for no entanglement, such as alternative modern psychologies postulate, with the microdynamics of body and brain, nor with the contingency that these, and not "mind-stuff," are a mind's correlates and antecedents. Nor does the electrical nature of this microdynamic hold any meaning for psychoanalytical theory and practice.

Of course, these exclusions or omissions are defended. The most intimate explorations of the live brain and nervous system have still not brought to light any indication that the flash, glow, and vanishment of an awareness follow from, and do not simply follow, its microdynamic occasions. Thus, regarding the necessary connection between consciousness and them, information from psychoneurology, neurophysiology, anatomy, and surgery can stir up belief but not yet present reliable knowledge. Current opinion holds that consciousness varies with the regions of brain action, that it alters as the brain changes and vanishes when the brain tires or breaks down, temporarily or for good. Among the known antecedents of breakdown or arrest of action are lack of glucose, scarcity of oxygen or vitamin B, concussions, anaesthetics and narcotics, whatever brings on fainting fits, epileptic seizures or othe disturbances of brain-function.

These antecedants are catastrophic. But there are other occasions when consciousness fades or vanishes which are regular events of the organism's daily round. The best-known is, of course, sleep, dreamful or dreamless. On the face of it, the sleeping life and the waking life are antithetical—as Socrates, waiting to drink the hemlock, long ago observed and concluded, hence, that body and soul are foes, that the life of the soul is a struggle to free itself from the shackles of the body and thus a lifelong pursuit of death.

While traditional religion clings to this conclusion, our sciences of body and mind draw other inferences. For, studying the microdynamics of their relationships, the sciences find brain and nervous system possessing the traits of a wet-cell battery. They find that what happens in them is a sequence of electrical events. They have distinguished in the composition of brain cells at least twelve elements: hydrogen, oxygen, nitrogen, carbon, phosphorous, sulphur, sodium, potassium, calcium, chlorine, iron, and magnesium. They opine that the intramolecular relations of these elements eventuate in tiny pulsations of electric current following each other in the brain and along the nerves, and that their sequence forms a "chain-reaction" wherein brain and nervous system discharge their organic functions with respect to the economy of the whole body (Cannon's "wisdom of the body") as a self-preserving organism. On several levels this is a reflex or autonomic economy, a homeostasis in which consciousness does not figure. The goings-on consist of a succession of emptyings and refillings, alternations of beats and rests, tensions and relaxations, such as the heart lives in. These seem to be regulated at the medulla. On this level, too, the body's economy is maintained by way of responses to outer stimuli, reflex actions fired at ganglia of the spinal cord. Then there ensues the level at which the wisdom of the body involves the play of consciousness. Here occur all those movements which are felt as voluntary, movements whose happening or not-happening is not a foregone conclusion. Their initiation and inhibition are attributed to the cerebellum. All the goings-on, voluntary and not, eventuate—sometimes together in a sort of teamwork and sometimes without apparent regard to one another.

At the topmost level, the cerebrum—literally, topmost, so that some authorities call this thin convoluted layer of gray matter the "roof-brain"—, the electric flash and flow correlate specifically to whatever we usually mean by "mind": memory, symbolization, association, imagination, reflection, reveries, decision, purpose, and plan. With the roof-brain's activities consciousness streams in all its diversifications—its waves and whirls, rapids and stillwaters, with their thrash and thump and foam and spindrift all orchestrating somehow into the singular "personal mind." Through every part of the nerve-tissue flows the bloodstream laving them, bringing them oxygen and sugar, and by its flow conditioning to speedup or slowdown the tiny, tiny nerve-current and brain current. The span and the range of consciousness coincide with the extent and depth of the "roof-brain" in electric play: the conscious actions of lips and tongue, of fingers and hands, involve more brain activity than the movements of the legs. So do those of the sense-organs.

Recording devices nowadays transpose electric brain-events into "encephalographs" and other such projections. These indicate that sleep is also electric, and that the difference between waking and sleeping goes with a difference of electric pulse or beat. When the eyes close and looking stops, the brain-waves projected from the visual center at the back of the head are steady and follow each other at the rate of ten beats a second. When the eyes are open and seeing, the sequence and tempo become irregular. During sleep, the sequence falls to three a second, and if the sleep becomes deep enough, the waves stop. They stop also when visual stimuli, from whatever source, are cut off. Such cutting off has been attributed to a center in the thalamus which operates like a guardian of this normal phase of cerebral rest and restoration whose name is sleep, and whose care and providence the ancients assigned to a god.

Complete stoppage of the electric brain-pulse is not required for normal sleep. On the contrary, some brain-cells go on flashing, as the cells of the heart go on beating, without being sparked from the senses or the skin. Moreover, all the body's cells—of the muscles, and of the glands as well as of nerves and brain—sustain a certain persistent tone or stretch, a posture of activity without action, below which inter-cellular transactions as well as transactions with the multitudinous world beyond the skin do not take place. Their taking place is marked by an intensifying speedup wherein plateaus of brain-activity heighten into the ups and downs of action. Death is the condition of complete atonicity and of no transactions whatever: sleep, narcosis, and the like sustain some tonus and some transactions. In intercellular terms, the number and variety of transactions of a living body are beyond counting. Electrical devices projecting them as sights or transposing them into sound have recorded nerve-currents of one-thousandth of a volt flowing at the rate of one ten-thousandth of a second.

11. Why the Mind Has A Body, Why the Body Has a Mind

Experience or awareness has for its immediate occasion or precondition this singular set or posture of the ever-mobilized cells of the cerebrum called tonus; it is their readiness to go off in linked electrical action upon impact from the senses. The linkings are incalculable. As the charges flow and spurt from cell to cell of the outer skin of the nerve cables, and across the synapses of neurone and dendrone of the roof-brain cells, their passage produces an undenumerable sequence of configurations, open and closed. How consciousness consummates these sequences of transfinite electrochemical and thermal events remains still undiscerned, and must so remain as long as the ancient riddle of the relation of mind to body is propounded in the form of Algernon Strong's question: *Why the mind has a body?* But ways to discernment open up if the query is given the form: *Why does the body have a mind?*

For, once the questioner takes for his center of reference what all experience exhibits and all records recount and appraise, the rôle of the mind in the body's history becomes apparent. The body is experienced, studied, and understood as an organic teamplay of a diversity of components whose transactions with one another impattern them into a whole where each more or less "fits" with all, and all with each. The "integration" due to the reciprocal fitting is by no means stable. It is ever strained by centrifugal or separatist trends within; it is ever under aggression by multitudinous patterned and unpatterned energies pushing in from the circumambient aggregates without. To keep itself going as a team, the body's existence must be a teamplay struggling to restore its inner losses and to heighten its inner cohesions (the concept of homeostasis was devised to provide one interpretation of all varieties of such restorative struggle).

Eating, drinking, sheltering, are names for the commonest restorative functions which, to be exercised, must at the same time be protected against attack from without. Self-protection is a critical activity of the body's struggle for survival. It can be achieved by flight or by defense, and both may occur as blind reflexes or conscious transactions. Reflexes are instant, like the jerking of its limb by Galvani's decapitated frog. Conscious transactions tend to become stretched-out events, involving some feeling of means and ends. The initiation of a conscious protective transaction is pain. Indeed, it has been argued that essential consciousness, consciousness *an und für sich* is but pain and its diversifications. Writers point out that actual physical hurt, even hurt which kills, can come with no pain, and that strong pain comes often with no discernible physical hurt. It was once argued that the body is stippled with sensitivities to pain and only pain. Studies of the nature and mechanism of pain and pain-experiences such as those of Livingston, of Nurry, and of many others, show this to be a mistaken hypothesis. Not only anaesthetic drugs such as the sick-room and the surgery employ, also taking thought can extinguish pain, and does so without reducing injury or insuring against its disastrous consequences. Different cultures take different attitudes toward pain, and there are religious cults whose entire rite and rote are postulated on dogmas of the unreality of pain; even as the sciences and arts of medicine, social hygiene, public health, both the allowed

and the disallowed, are among the notable positive consequences of pain. So, often, are laughing and weeping,
which pain can initiate and pervasively qualify.

Unlike pain, pleasure is rarely localized or related to
specific nerve-ends. Pleasure may be experienced with any
intro- or extro-somatic activity, adient or abient. In abient
experiences it is often identified as relief from pain; and
again, as the sequence of returning consciousness from
an unconscious state, even if the return is ultimately the
reinauguration of pain. The reports of awakeners from
the anaesthesia of a knockout, a dental operation, or some
major surgery, suggest an unsought consensus on this
theme. Mystics, too, indicate that the feeling of pleasure
is the positive initiation of either the mystic sleep or the
mystic awakening from the unutterably ineffable mystic
perception—the "anaesthetic revelation," whether religious or secular. Like pain, pleasure can suffuse with its
own characteristic timbre both laughter and tears. Each
pulse of it has rise, climax, and exhaustion singular to
itself, making up a specific stretch of wholeness or health,
a moment of euphoria and quantum of well-being.

Like pain, pleasure initiates in a conscious transaction
comprehending a sequence of ends and means, often
composing a conspectus of them. The conspectus tends to
diversify and build up into a personal history a sustained
feeling of goal and going. Wherever this feeling is articulated in words and other symbols and the articulation
affirmed as a life-plan, it may be called "the pursuit of
happiness." And often the dominant program of the
pursuit becomes the control and elimination of the causes
of pain, and thus, in extension, a war against "evil." Many
philosophies appraise the human enterprise everywhere
as a confrontation of "the problem of evil," and transpose

the pursuit of happiness into a hunting down and extirpation of evil. Therewith the play of laughter and tears changes from a personal reaction into a cultural configuration, and the "field" of a value-system.

12. Memory, Survival, and Extinction

Every individual pulse of the tidal give-and-take between *I* and *me-here*, *I* and *you-there*, *I* and *that-there*, which signalizes the insurgence of the "subject"-"object" consciousness, takes a stretch of time delimitable by the space it traverses. For the most part, minimal body-brain transactions via the nervous system take from a tenth-of-a-second to a second, more or less, to complete themselves. Their doing this follows from the fact that the electric impulses which consciousness consummates, move from any inner or outer end-organ to their cortical terminal or vice versa, at a rate of from three to thirty meters a second inclusive of the critical pause of perhaps one three-thousandths of a second at the synaptic gaps between the brain-cells.

In certain cells, of course, impulses also fuse and persist, forming currents which so shape an orbit joining groups of cells together as to form a "closed circuit." If a sensory impulse should draw such a group into a new configuration, the group would recover its autonomy via the intra-cellular sodium-potassium process. Certain writers ascribe memory to these "closed circuits" and appraise them as self-preserving recordings of a person's every single experience, recalled or unrecalled. They hold the circuits to keep forming till the day we die and to preserve the changes of self we call learning. Sense-impressions bring them mostly into play as critical parts of the ideo-motor responses which fuse and shape all our perceptions. The responses, far more than the impressions, qualify the *what* of perception, however it bears on the self-preservation of the perceiver.

For the impressions pour upon the brain in uncountable multitudes, and investigators have so far not found any instance of a one-one correspondence between neural pattern and any circumambient physical eventuation or psychosomatic formation. They have not found any specific, invariant co-ordination between perceptual quality and brain area. They have noted that an impact at the visual areas, or at the center of the muscle-sense, may be followed by not only the conventionally to-be-expected response, but also by experiences of touch, or temperature, or pain, or postural feeling, or pressure, or movement, or color—separate or all together. The transactions are variables, and what mode of experience consummates them seems to decide itself during that unperceived, imperceptible, yet measurable pause at the synapses. During this pause, shall we say, some phase of the livingly conserved past is presently in play. It is a phase ready and alert but not a-go. As the body receives the impacts of the world without, this stretch of past installs itself "homeostatically" in the alterative event, thus to keep up the teaming and teamplay of organs while they are changing relationships and entering into new formations.

The current word for this always compounding sequence of transactions is "feedback." In terms of feedback, perception would be such an ongoing living penetration by the past into the eventuating present as prophetically to shape it toward the future. This would render perception a succession of choices and decisions among alternative actions such as approaching and avoiding, containing and extruding, enveloping and repelling, fixating, attending and indifferently bypassing, and so on. Whatever alternative configurations do take shape remain unclosed until what the late Edward Thorndike called "the confirming reaction" accomplishes closure and establishes decision.

Concerning this reaction Thorndike wrote in *Man and His Works,*

> it acts biologically, not logically . . . more like a hormone than like a syllogism. . . . You do not have a dozen a week, or a dozen a day, but more nearly a dozen a minute. . . . It has its source in the over all control of a person at the time . . . has its origin outside the situation-response units upon which its acts . . . may be in some cases the act of a free agent, a free will, in the most useful sense of these words. . . . To some extent man modifies himself. The confirming reaction is issued by a man when the man is satisfied. The man originates as a certain collection or battery or outfit of genes which is by definition and hypothesis apart from and contrasted with its environment. Day by day that man has changed his nature partly by the influence of his own confirmations of connections whose consequences satisfy him. Each person is to that extent an *imperium in imperio naturae.* Each person is a center of creative force modifying himself more or less to suit himself.

This confirming reaction would seem to be intrinsic to the *what* of experience. Without it, apparently, nothing is learned, nothing forgotten; the transactional sequences of stimulus-response spread out unshaped. With it, an order sets itself up, a structure develops of attitudes, of habits of preference and rejection, of pursuit, capture and mastery, of fight and subordination, compounding the undenumerable items of personal experience into the singularity of at once a psychosomatic character now present and a personal history sequentially making itself.

The locus of this making is the moving frontier where self and world compenetrate in the transactions usually called learnings; it is where the "confirming reaction" bets past experience on future change. Perception is the decisive phase of this wager, and each percipient makes a somewhat different bet.

13. Logic, Liberty, and Memory

Such also may be said to be the conclusion of mathematical logicians who have been questing after certainty and extend this finding to the certitudes of arithmetic insofar as that art is purely logical and not ideomotor and consequential. In the history of the matter, the issues under consideration began with belief in the infallibility of the rationalist's "reflexive argument." After a time, they were transferred to the no less rationalistic challenge of infallibility by the contradiction intrinsic to the idea of a "class of all classes." Their current formation is known as "Gödel's theorem." Gödel purports to establish that a proposition which can be derived from the basic postulates (i.e., articles of faith) upon which any system is constructed cannot serve to disclose that this system does not hide inconsistencies and self-contradition. If, moreover, a different system is used to establish the self-consistency of the first one, then Gödel's theorem applies to the second one, and so on to the third and fourth, *ad infinitum*. The consequence? That it is not logical proof but a "confirming reaction" which supports logical certainty.

Now the reaction is an act of faith, an ideo-motor commitment to a bet which can never be a bet on a sure thing. "Certainty" denotes what Adelbert Ames calls "the weighted average of past experience," a gauge of probabilities built, checked, and modified by actions in an ongoing summation of feedbacks whose reciprocal suffusion compounds into the substance of purpose and its realizing processes. That none of these can be foregone conclusions, that all presume the intervention of an unpredictable and undesirable component, a factor of freedom, becomes a very hopeful working postulate, if consciousness be in fact a spontaneous variation from a sequence of interneuronic electro-chemical transactions. For brain-activity engages some ten billion neurones; its electrical impulses follow each other in such numbers and in such a number and variety of their combinations, and can occasion during any person's life-span such an uncountable procession of diverse conscious states, that both impulses and states might require denoting in transfinite powers of transfinite numbers.

Persons who are able to catch bit glimpses of the rocketlike jettings and jettisonings that compenetrate into the stream of their own consciousness also sense how much eventuates and how little of it persists. The spontaneous variations of the mind occur with infinite abundance; what of them survives and does not perish is by contrast finite to scarcity. An unceasing selection goes on, whereof perhaps a diversifying homeostatic process produces the gradient. Along this the originalities, the innovations, the inventions, the discoveries are naturalized or alienated by the confirming reaction according as they themselves are felt to confirm and expand, to repattern and transmute, or to weaken and disperse the formations they arise among. Percepts, and concepts which are the latest residues of percepts confluent, ingathered, abstracted, and symbolized, seem in this respect on a par. In both, the diversified play of past experience in present response links immediate stimulation, from whatever source, with residues of other times and other places. The linkage transvalues them into prophecies of the shape of things to come and frees personality from isolation in immediacy.

Inasmuch as the uniting of sensory presence to sensory absence, which the linkage performs, is memory-at-work, memories are disclosed as the energies of freedom, and their creation and accumulation, which we call learning, are the unceasing pursuit of liberty. Without the processes of remembering, perception could not happen nor conception eventuate. Memory is the vital function whereby the person's mind re-enforces his synergic struggle to go on struggling which is the all of his being alive and not dead. But whether that function is successfully exercised remains an ever-open question whose closure is in one context "animal faith"; in another, "will-to-believe-at-the-believer's-own-risk." The closure is a bet whose winning or losing consummates not the data of the wager, but the hypothetical future sequences projected from the data.

14. The Role of the Senses and the Brain in the Production of Personality

The events which we mostly think and imagine are visual. Mankind is pre-eminently an eye-minded species, and all our terms for prehension, understanding, rationality, and the like, are variously signals for seeing and the seen—insight, vision, theory, being such more literally.

To say of a person that he is a man of vision is to approve him; to declare that he is without vision is to disqualify him. Blindness is appraised as a greater handicap than deafness, while insensitivity to touch, taste, and smell are often regarded as advantages in the overcoming of certain situations. In view of the boundless range of the impacts upon our sensorium, all our sense organs function within narrow limits of stimulation. Events below those limits evoke no response; above them, they produce unpleasant-ness, discomfort, pain, disordered response, and ultimately destruction of the responding organ. However impacts above or below the limits of sensibility may be qualified— tactile, gustatory, olfactory, thermal, auditory, visual, kinesthetic—they all are processes and eventuations; they have each its own singularity of tension or vibration or movement, capable of being diminished or increased. Hence, they can be brought within the limits of ex-perience by means of devices which transmute them sometimes into auditory, mostly into visual events. (As-tronomers' employment of such devices disclosed tradi-tion's unheard music of the spheres to be, when rendered audible, a somewhat unpleasant noise.) The effect is to render knowledge, more than anything else, sequences seen, heard, symbolized, recorded, arrested, repeated, and stored in books and tapes, films and microfilms. Touch, taste, temperature, posture, push, pull, balance, remain ongoing experiences never to be detached from feeling as are sight and sound. Severally and jointly, they are next-to-next actions called "contact." They are feeling *in actu*, the stuff of feeling. Their changing relational patterns, consummating as our postures and attitudes, may all be qualified by laughter or tears, and expressed with images and words. Love or hate, fear, anger or rage, disgust, delight or joy, elation or depression, panic or ecstacy, are among our names for these diversely adient or abient intrasomatic tensions; while emotion is our name for all of them together.

In the context of brain-body relations, emotion presents certain overall somatic resemblances to the roof-brain's intra-cellular readiness of response which precedes articulate awareness. Emotion discloses itself as unarticulated awareness about to pass over into articulating action. It appears to consist of transactions engaging neuro- muscular tonus, ready to detonate in action, but action without form, direction, or goal, unless the detonation be itself the goal. And the latter seems to be the case. For emotion expresses itself in unordered bursts, not in ordered sequences. We not uncommonly qualify it as "blind." Love is "blind." Persons are said to be "blinded" by rage or fear or jealousy, and so on. Emotion not expressed in gradient motion is appraised as pathological and destructive.

There is a wide consensus that feeling had best come out in formed action. When its ideo-motor release is patterned to objects of the world without or of the mind within, values are born; things and thoughts and persons are qualified as good or bad, right or wrong, beautiful or ugly, tragic or comic, and the qualifications overflow the entire felt network of transactions wherein those objects figure. Such overflows are said to convert blindness into vision: for example, the philosophic tradition since Plato celebrates love as the pursuit of wisdom consummating in the vision of ideal reality.

Yet vision is by no means the most human of our senses, nor the most filiative or separative in our relations with one another. There is reason to believe that in these respects hearing holds precedence over seeing. True, the eye reaches farther than the ear. But farther less significantly. Things seen are experienced more as forms than formations, as presences more than passages. They look more static and are felt as more stable. We distinguish them with less effort than things heard. Recall and recognition alter them less. We see them quite unaware of the media and manner of seeing, and should we want not to see them, we can shut our eyes or turn our backs or put out the light. Indeed, the position of the eyes and the limited range of turning for the head also confine the field of seeing to whatever the eyes can take in within an angle of about 120 degrees. Vision ends at our shoulders. We are cut off by our build from seeing what is behind us.

The case is different with hearing. If we are not deaf, sound reaches our ears not only as light reaches our eyes, from in front, but also from behind, from above, from beneath, from within, from all around. Even in sleep we can no more get away from sound than we can get away from ourselves. Moreover, we experience it not as formed presence but as passing formation. Sequent movement, rhythmic and arhythmic, patterned and unpatterned, is of its substance and we so experience it, and determine the experience to be noise, music, speech, or outcry. Sound comes to us from our hearts beating, our lungs breathing, and from all the movements of things seen and things not-seen that stir the air around into airwaves which the ear can translate into sound; while what the ear cannot translate the entire body feels as a consequential thrust of movements following one after the other and compounding. The movements have mass, weight, direction and are of the stuff of sound's sensory concreteness. Their auditory innateness defeats the mind's every effort to fix, to hold, or to rest upon any movement of sound. What we look at, we can see as it seems, in itself and by itself; we can look at it for its own sake, without taking it as a sign of anything else, and without any conscious care for its cause or consequence. There it is, and for the nonce, all there is. Not so with our hearings. Even when we listen to music, we tend to refer the sounds to a source and to project them toward a consequence other than what they are in themselves and by themselves. We tend to take them for signs and meanings of less mobile, more persistent existences, threatening survival or promising safety. The rôle of sound as such in alerting consciousness is more direct, closer to feeling and action, less interwoven with symbolic reference than the rôle of sight. But at the same time it is a rôle more immediately suitable for carrying meanings. For it is the constant accompaniment of both the overt and subliminal changing of psycho-somatic postures, attitudes, and movements. Be the sounds we make those we want to make or can't help making, our ears hear them, accept, reject, and insofar as they are amenable to conscious control, remember, repeat, and regulate them. In due course, they become speech and song. Soon or late they are associated with visible images and signs. Tonguing, seeing, and hearing get orchestrated into literate language, and laughter and tears are largely phonations.

So, although adult people do not focus selfhood in their belches and burps, they do focus it, far more than they are commonly aware, in the ever changing tonus of voice and speech. To an astonishing degree, self-conscious-ness is voice-consciousness, subvocal talking; a man's character and personality are more signalized by the pitch, rhythm, and volume of his voice than by the meanings he voices. The words he uses and his phonations in using them express the style of his being, the modes of his teaming-up with other men, and the gradient of his personal history.

None of the nine muses, even Terpsichore, presides over a silent art; nor is there any known silent science. The life of all is communication, whose energies flow from the ongoing synergy of signatory sound-making and sound-hearing which we call language. Indeed, on the free flow of this synergy of signification depends the cohesion of every team of humans and every society and every culture. Speech is spirit, and "the style is the man." Genetically, *logos* is the flesh made *word*, which consciousness readily enough inverts into the word made flesh. For *logos* in consciousness is the unseen and invisible made known by the hearing of the ear. St. Paul wrote to his Romans: "Faith must come from what is heard" (Rom. X,ii) and that passing sound, whose passage is evidence of things not seen, comes to silence at last in the visible presence of the unseen, consummating faith in fact. The visible is the stable, unmoving form and to it is attributed a permanence that resists all alteration and that sets at naught all forces of change. It is endowed with the impenetrability which the sense of touch, of all senses, most reliably conveys, and which bespeaks the Ultima Thule of whatever we mean by "matter." The world of unseen spirit that faith attests, evinces when brought to vision, the qualitative differentia of tangible matter whereof fact is presumed to consist—inalterability, impenetrability. This would signalize matter as spirit-at-rest; spirit as matter-in-motion.

Spirit and matter, then, may be but names for diversifying phases of an ongoing process, the phases reciprocally compenetrative and interchangeable. The relationships become notably significant in terms of brain-body transactions, of the bearing of sense on intellect and on intelligence, and of all these on the self-forming concretions of the human kind and their diverse cultures. For the import of the relationships is that no person need depend for his humanity on any one sense alone, so long as the sense he has available can serve him as a means of communication with individuals who do have the more desirable sensibilities of ear and eye and the power of speech. The indispensable organ of his humanity would then appear to be the roof-brain with its functions of selective association and orchestration, replacement and signification.

Now detailed study of the roof-brain discloses that with adequate supplies of oxygen and sugar it works in and with the body as a considerably independent variable; it does its stuff also when unspurred by impulses from the proprioceptive and extero-ceptive organs of the body.

Among the most moving and meaningful verifications of this observation is, of course, the personal history of Helen Keller, which signalized for William James a blessing upon darkness-burdened and fear-encumbered mankind. Immediate experience for Helen Keller is tactile experience only. From the age of two, sightless, soundless, and thereby mute, she receives the impacts from the world around only through her fingers and feet, her skin and bones and muscles. All Miss Keller's empathies are perforce tactile empathies. She has with great pains learned to speak a little. But while it is wonderful, it is not comfortable to hear her. For even the sounds she might automatically produce she can do little to control, refine and improve, since she has no hearing to check them with. Nor the actualities of light, color, and visual form, of noises, music, and speech, nor the configurations of ideas can ever come to her in direct prehensions. They can never be her face-to-face acquaintances. She lacks the organs of their intuition. Her knowledge of them must remain, so long as she lives, knowledge-about, symbolic, and indirect.

Directly, it can consist of nothing else than kinesthetic tactilities which people retaining all their senses would think of as inconceivably refined, discriminated, and orchestrated—a procession of ordered touch-movement sequences betokening the grammar of speech and the grammar of visible and audible existence; systems of predicates, each an organon qualifying inalterably transcendental subjects. The speed, intensity, and organizational patterns of these signalizing and communication systems may be inferred from the same traits of expert fingering of musical instruments such as a piano, a clarinet, or a violin played by a virtuoso with his eyes shut. The systems' formations and functions come very near to those of the audio-visual symbol systems wherewith mathematical physicists bespeak the inter-dynamics of atoms and the intra-particulate relationships which lie beyond all human sensibilities. Miss Keller, in steady communication with a guide and teacher all of whose senses were intact, learned to transpose animal and human forms and features into tactile sequences, each a specific configuration shaping into a uniqueness of its own singularities of mass, motion, texture, firmness, or fluidity, wetness or dryness, scent and vibrational individuality. By laying her fingers on a speaker's or singer's voice-box, she experiences the diverse timbres and pitches which orchestrate into his individual voices, but the voice is beyond her power to experience. Musical compositions come to her as vibrations on the floor whose sequences she discriminates and compounds as they reach her brain from her feet: she "listens with her feet."

But none of these immediacies of touch and movement could be any more than passages of feeling unless they were lastingly co-ordinated with signs and symbols composing a language. Motions of vocal chords and tongue had to be translated into motions of fingers, responses of the ear replaced by such responses of the palm of the hand that touch might signify as hearing signifies. For Miss Keller, although she has learned to speak and could say to reporters, "I am no longer dumb," language is tactile. Touches, composed into swift sequences that the palm of the hand at last had learned to discriminate and recognize, made up grammatical patterns communicated by moving fingers. Each pattern had to be learned and brought into meaningful relationships with others, until whole books could be spelled out into the hand. Ultimately it became feasible to transpose these into Braille and to repeat the transpositions on a typewriter. Next steps were from a system of tactile surrogates for speech in English to similar ones in French, German, and Latin; from identification of these concrete differences of sign into conceptual abstractions and philosophical ideas.

We have here discrimination and organization of tactilities and kinesthesias into a universe of discourse symbolizing persons and places, attitudes, thoughts, and things. And we have them meaning objects and events and relations like those that the languages of many-sensed people mean. This remarkable achievement would be impossible without the selective and orchestrating work of a highly-ready, delicately-triggered roof-brain. The entirety of Miss Keller's magnificent adventure in making herself which is her education is simultaneously also her liberation. Her personal history uniquely embodies the pursuit of liberty whereof the struggle to go on struggling consists. It spans one brave, uncheckable crossing of boundary after boundary, an unrelaxed widening and deepening of a pitifully narrow world and thereby the creation and perception of an ever-growing self.

Helen Keller's motor equipment remained unimpaired when she lost her sight and hearing, and Anne Sullivan mobilized her little pupil's powers of discriminative and interpretative movement by guiding her experiences into geometrically compounding sequences of tactile and kinesthetic impressions, series of which she could, in recollection, use as signs and symbols of other series. The symbolic and signifying ones thus became Miss Keller's ideas of an unseen and unheard world of goings-on; they became also her ways of pooling that world with the other worlds of sight and sound into one shared with hearers and see-ers. She was even brought to speech, though in a toneless, high-pitched voice which discloses the lack of the ear's modulating co-operation.

The story of Douglas Robert Steuart Bader takes a different but as singular a turn. As Paul Brickhill tells it in *Reach for the Sky*, this hero of the Battle of Britain and ace of World War II grew to a harmonious psychosomatic manhood with all his senses and all his limbs. But in 1931 an airplane accident cost him both his legs. His right leg had to be amputated at the thigh, his left at the knee. He was then twenty-one years old. A Royal Air Force Hospital finally provided him with mechanical legs with which he at last learned not only to walk, but to play golf and squash, to dance, and to turn somersaults. Of course the peacetime air force treated him as ineligible to service, but the war-emergency altered the rules. Once again in the Force, his skill and daring in handling a fighter-plane earned a D.F.C. and a D.S.C. and the rank of colonel. Shot down, the Nazis captured and jailed him, but he manoeuvered so many escapes that they first deprived him of his prosthetic limbs, and finally sent him to Kolditz where they kept him prisoner until the fighting stopped in Europe. He is now an executive of the Shell Oil Company and still flying.

To date I have seen no report of any study of the psychosomatic processes whereby artificial limbs were drawn into dynamic configuration with the remnants of Col. Bader's natural ones, and with his entire body. If one exists, I do not know it. An inquirer can only guess at what happened.

Would it be going far afield to conjecture that, of the varieties of living organisms whose power of regrowing lost limbs has disappeared with their becoming mammals, man is the only one able to compensate this biological deprivation by fabricating inanimate mechanical devices which he attaches to his living flesh and works as he might the lost part? The first guess would be that man has devised inanimate surrogates to perform the vital functions not of feet and hands alone, but of internal organs as well. The naturalization of metals, plastics, and other materials in the place of bone and flesh as working units of the somatic team obviously consummates a process of learning. It implies a field of ideo-motor tension, of patterned readiness into which unnatural matter is conformed, perhaps like iron-filings by a magnetic field. That such a field may be more than a postulate is suggested by the experiences of discomfort, pain, and movement which amputees of all times are reported to localize in limbs they no longer possess. Learning the functional incorporation of artificial ones might well consist of a homeostatic sequence projecting stored ideo-motor images into the surrogate while the new activities of muscles and nerves are presenting immediate experiences with which the remembered patterns at last orchestrate and become confluent, by dint of an extended and deepened feedback.

As with Helen Keller, the process of education is a process of liberation, a passage from immobility and dependence to mobile independence. Commitment to it is commitment to the pursuit of liberty. Indispensable to the learner's catching up with liberty, to his consummating learning in habits of smooth, economical, and purposeful movement that shall make a part of the ever-changing configurations of the struggle to go on struggling which compose his, the learner's, personal history, is his will to acquire the habits and his faith that he can acquire them. This could be animal faith alone. But in human company it is an open bet which the learner makes with himself and with his neighbors on an undertaking whose success can have no guarantee, even in his own will-to-believe. A more traditional word for this wager is courage, and Mr. Brickhill rightly signalizes the will-to-believe initiating Douglas Bader's self-liberation as "showing humanity new horizons of courage, not in war, not only for the limbless, but in life."

When fortune intruded upon Douglas Bader the task of shaping himself anew to a wholeness orchestrated to his cultural pattern, he was already a man formed, his selfhood in full configuration with the lifespace of his community. But the history of the formation of Helen Keller's self is *ab initio* conscious social history: it is the

epic of intimate transactions between Helen Keller and
Anne Sullivan, Helen Keller and Polly Thompson, and
through them with persons, places, thoughts, and things
and their symbolic surrogates, anywhere in the world.
Miss Keller's legend is at once unique and representative,
heroic and betokening the human condition everywhere.
It signalizes the transactional nature of the self, and how
entirely and ineffably mind is a function of what is
minded by the body which minds it.

15. The Self of Self-Consciousness

In the light of the record here, and of every such
record, it becomes clear why Heraclitus had to fail when
he set out to seek himself without seeking the world;
why Socrates maneuvered himself into a blind alley when,
having decided that he could not know the world but
could know himself, he set out upon that quest for certitudes of self-knowledge which led away from all reliable
knowledge; why his pupil Plato had at last to identify
self and reality by asserting that mind holds immortal
possession of a hidden world of ideas always and everywhere the same, ideas which become unconscious memories at birth and are darkly envisioned and pursued and on
occasion recovered to consciousness during life. Plato
argued that self-knowledge is the full and exclusive consciousness of these unconsciously-held ideas. In addition
Plato postulated the attainment of this self-knowledge
on a social process of desocialization by means of compe-
titive intercommunication between different selves cham-
pioning different valuations of existence. The traditional
name for this process is "the Socratic method." Scholastic

disputation came on as a variation upon it by employing the semantics of Aristotle to serve the intentions of churchmen. The latter postulated the human condition as a transaction with God and the Devil based upon revealed knowledge of what the two want of mankind, of what nature enables mankind to do about it; and of how the supernatural wants are treated by the self's takings or refusals of the godly and satanic covenants.

The last, of course, could not be otherwise disclosed than as actions of the body. At their most disembodied they must needs still be a symbolic gesture or a speaking or writing of words. Since, however, gestures and speech and their feel are products coincident with their production, and since the efficacious processes of production go on underneath the skin, the products are experienced separately from their ongoing causes and occasions. They are experienced as action-patterns which the body subserves rather than as exercise of bodily functions. Duly they are combined into felt arrangements of images, sayings, and movements which echo, but are no longer prolongations of, the body and its projections and reverberations. In them we have the substance of what is intended by such words as "soul," "spirit" or "ghost." Perceptually, they are the body's surface, its boundary of face and form and selected functions, like a painter's portrait disconnected from the organs and activities going on beneath and behind.

So, the initial "self" of self-consciousness plays no major rôle in its makeup. We draw most of its componets from the attitudes and actions of other persons— when in our bodily presence. Our ideas of our selves develop upon selective refractions from those presences, supplemented by mirror-images from inanimate reflectors, including photographs. Rarely do they comprehend the organic formations of work beneath the skin on whose synergy consciousness supervenes, and whose functions it supplements, adjusts, and re-enforces—or aborts. Every seeing man's image of his own personality tends thus to be ghostly—a visual image nourished, projected, shaped, and reshaped by means of the body's struggling among other bodies, by its minding them in order to mind its own survival and enhancement as struggle. What any discerns of those others, it then by means of symbols assimilates into his own image of himself. Invisible impulsions from invisible heart and kidney and glands and brain and viscera and muscles somehow get into topological configuration with visible body-pattern and unlocalized tactile and kinesthetic feeling. The span of self-consciousness stretches somatically: self is experienced not only at the boundary of outer perception where body and environment encounter, but also within the bounds of the tactile and kinesthetic patterns rising as transactions between intra-somatic parts.

The conscious image of self which thus eventuates is rarely reported, even by neurophysiologists and neuropsychologists. It continues to belong to a consensus still to be reached by a remote world to come, if any. As signalizing this image, the word "self" is a verb, not a noun. It stands for a process of self-ing. It signifies an ongoing sequence of interchanges between visceral, glandular, and neuromuscular activities orchestrating into selectively patterned transactions with circumambient diversities of gravity, air, water, light, and what not in their mobilities and inertias. It signifies this sequence consummating as the ideo-motor imagery for which the general term is "perception." It signifies this consummation, however perception be appraised—sane, insane, realistic, illusory, hallucinational, fantastic, true, false. Whatever its appraisal may be postulated upon—be it introsomatic chemistry, normal or abnormal (such as the drug is currently assumed to produce whose effects resemble schizophrenia—lysergic acid, LSO), be it the impact of poisons or narcotics, be it the impact of persons and places— perception consummates the consequent transaction. But the sane does not distinguish itself from the insane, nor the realistic from the illusory by what it is in itself. These distinctions are consequences of the action which percepts lead to; the success or failure of the perceiver's bet on their import for his future. In both cases perception will pass over into either the unconscious but ever active muscular memory which the word "habit" signifies or into the visual, aural, and other conscious formations whose propulsions as awareness we call "remembering," "recollection," "recognition," and whose variations, deviants, and spontaneities we call "imagination." The entire spiralling orchestration becomes the psychosomatic formation to which the words "character," "personality," "temperament," are often interchangeably applied.

16. Man's Two Wisdoms

We perceive the process in others as a certain ideomotor set or posture, imparting its singularity to their audio-visual presence. We feel it to be in ourselves, and as ourselves, an ineffable intimate readiness for the transactions of self-preservation, an ongoing indefeasible formation of attitudes and stance which persistently resists upsetting, resets when upset, and enlarges its base and

range as a tree thrusts its roots farther and deeper into
the nourishing earth while its trunk and branches push
upward and outward to the sun and air. The rooted tree
and the mobile man are both reaching after upkeep and
support. Cannon called the unconscious phase of this
entire process "the wisdom of the body." The conscious
phase might similarly be called "the wisdom of the
mind"; but tradition calls it "reason," "reflection," "learning," "habituation."

Developmentally, the two wisdoms orchestrate
enough to re-enforce one another, and their configuration
and survival as a team consummates their synergy. Of
this we have sufficient evidence in the diffusion of *species
humanum* over every part of the earth's surface, in the
growth of its power to resist and to master all sorts and
conditions of rival species and much of inanimate nature
itself. But there is also the parallel record of the inhumanity of men to themselves and to their own likes,
which points to a certain divergence and separation of the
two wisdoms from each other, to a warfare of the two
wisdoms. The record suggests that the mind's genesis
and justification as an organ of the self-preserving body's
organs of survival are being negated and its vital function
atrophied and inverted. For example, many religions
cultivate an economy postulated on the idea that the
survival of the self is the survival of an audio-visual ghost
of the body; that the wellbeing of the body is the foe of
the wellbeing of the ghost; that to have a care for the
body's wellbeing is to commit unpardonable sin and to be
tainted with ineradicable guilt; that immortal life for
the ghost depends on the killing of the body, on the
"mortification of the flesh." Toward the turn of the century, Sigmund Freud transposed these appraisals of

human nature into the constructs of his psychology, and the schools of psychoanalysis which variously derive from his postulates have kept this transposition the ground of their disciplines. However else they may differ, they preserve a consensus regarding the tensional stratification of the psyche, the dynamics of the conflict between its strata, the consequent relations between repressive-super-egoic force and expressive-desiring-idic fraud and re-garding what the relations between the force and fraud work out in the formation of the struggling ego with its guilt-feelings, its fears, its anxieties, its projections, its rationalizations and its sublimations.

Not much in these formations is presented in tactile or kinesthetic terms. Except, perhaps, for laughter and tears, they are mostly set forth as visual sequences, verbal-ized. Yet, it is by the divergence between *what* is said and *how* it is said that the warfare between body and spirit is laid bare. For in the light of the neurophysiolo-gist's disclosures, the spirit is flesh made word and per-ceived without regard to its ground and occasion. All sensory and lower association centres contribute to the action of the nerve base and of the speech centres. Much of what Plato has to say in the *Cratylus*, the reports of a long line of analysts who explored the soundings-off of poets and orators, can be brought back to changes of the body's stance and alterations of muscle tonus and breath-ing in respiratory organs and voice-box. Alarm and security, pain and delight, anxiety and repose, all go with an initially somatic specificity of phonation which the ear hears and processes. Each sound, even as our coughs and gasps, our groans and hisses, our sneezes and snorts, our laughings and weepings, goes with body movements from one posture to another, started, stopped, completed, either singly or in different patterns of togetherness. Each sound may be automatic or voluntary. If voluntary, it need bear no functional relation to the bodily need it serves as automatic. Soon or late all sounds may become, as products of our voice-production mechanism, variables independent of their first springs and occasions, suggesting them by the phonations they are, yet meaning something else, perhaps vastly else, with which they have come to belong by later association.

17. Man as a Warfare of His Two Wisdoms

Often the wisdom of the mind suppresses the wisdom of the body and shapes the body into conformation with its own image. This relationship is intrinsic to the human condition. For selves live as centers of transactions with other selves, as "social" dynamisms, and minds work for the most part as "social" effects of individuals in rivalry or teamplay or both. They mind one another regarding thoughts, things and consequences which they feel bear on their survival and its conditions, and each practices his reciprocated vigilance as the *sine qua non* of his own freedom and safety. In practically every culture, the resulting formations are such as the body's uncultured wisdom would not shape up; they are such as it tends to fend off and elude when shaped to them by the mind. The shaping, we must keep in mind, is not and cannot be that of an external power modelling an object other than itself. Difficult as the relationship may be to perceive, the shaping is like that of any other organ of the body, say the hand, pressing and kneading and pulling and twisting some other part. In nature, living bodies sustain a dynamic symmetry, a mobile equilibrium of organs and energies, singular to each.

A body's uncultivated stance, at whatever posture, seems always and everywhere set at the position of greatest mechanical advantage. Its "beauty" by nature rather than by culture is an effulgence from this position. But what culture does not cultivate quite another than this natural balance of the body and does not therewith redress the deformation and unbalancing rendered *de rigeur* by its creed and code? Taboos and prescriptions regarding garments and garniture, tatoos, paintings, scarifications, hair and head dressing; styles of standing, sitting, moving, lying, feeding, mating; work forms, play patterns, and most of resting—make up the best of manners and the highest of morals. They consolidate in personal habits and communal custom and they may debilitate physique and distort anatomy; they may corrupt the sensitivity of the senses and disable them from serving in the personality's exigent transactions with its surroundings. The sanctioned right, good, beautiful, and true may then be— as very widely it is—the neuropsychological wrong, evil, ugly, and false; inhibitory, frustrating, crippling. Whatever culture the sanctioned forms are values of, as wisdom of the mind they may be waging a chronic war, hot and cold, against the wisdom of the body, with consequences to both of enslavement, agony, guilt, and toil such as religions of disillusion and existentialist cults build their creeds and codes upon. Their tears are sardonic, their laughters bitter.

On the other hand, when a happy chance orchestrates the wisdom of the body and the wisdom of the mind into harmonious confluence, the personality's transactions with the world around may prosper or fail with no threat to its integrity. The world may press in upon it—pushing, pulling, twisting, bending, squeezing together, or yanking apart—or it may go the man's way, supporting and nour-ishing his intentions, releasing his energies, diverting what would obstruct, averting what would inhibit. With its dualized wisdom now re-orchestrated into psycho-somatic wholeness, the personality can sustain attack and not retreat, endure suffering and maintain itself in in-tegrity, while from friendly transactions it can draw nourishment and heightening. In either condition only this undivided inner freedom to react can be the reliable ground of the personality's outer security, and the security be such as will support the inner freedom.

18. Liberty, Process; Liberty, Substance

The upshot of all the foregoing observations would be that "pursuit of liberty" and "struggle for self-preserva-tion" are alternative expressions for the human condition. The word "liberty," like the word "self," is a verb before it is a noun. It signifies not a state or trait but an action going on. By first intention it means passage and relation, it points to both the diversity of inner transactions whose reciprocal determinations compound into a continuing personal identity and it points to the sequences of trans-actions between this identity and other such orchestrations, including non-personal events, thoughts, and things. By first intention *liberty*, in sum, signalizes those altering intra-organic relations whereby an organism stays a *live* organism as it carries on, its give-and-take being the on-going transaction of the self's inner concords and conflicts with the like relations between the diverse and diversifying surroundings outside. This activity is what the verb "liberty" denotes.

But usage hypostatizes the verb into a noun which is employed to name an endowment, a state or trait. The American Declaration of Independence pronounces liberty, together with life and the pursuit of happiness, to be unalienable rights—implying that life and liberty are endowments possessed, while happiness is a condition whose pursuit, not whose possession, is such an endowment. The Universal Declaration of Human Rights uses "rights and freedoms" as co-ordinate terms with different but overlapping meanings. Both declarations gives *liberty* or *freedom* substantive import. Even when the nouns are joined to such prepositions as "from," "of," "in," "to," "under," they signify a state or possession. In the light of present knowledge the distinction resembles that which physicists make between wave and particle, a distinction which turns on an inquirer's convenience in dealing with eventuations. The distinction does not signalize a disclosure of incommensurables eventuating. "Life and liberty," when used to signify endowments or possessions, mean the instant phase of the ongoing pursuit which we call "struggle for survival." However instant, it is still a stretch of time; it is still a span of successive quanta which form the past by compenetrating as they succeed one another, while the successions that recur contingently diversify as they recur. They come with innovations, each of which is coincidentally both a new determination in a field of indetermination and an alteration of an already determined past which thereby becomes the future of that past.

Perceived in their reciprocal compenetrations, the transactions which are life and liberty present themselves

substantively, as firm presences; envisioned as the succession of eaches, next to next, they are a process of pursuit, a becoming, by a coming after, of event upon event.
In immediate experience, substantive liberty is sequent
liberty self-consummated; it is pursuit totalizing itself
into possession; it is an ongoing eventuation of successive
goals whereof each is but a boundary and a sign-post in a
passage which is its own goal. If life, liberty, and the
pursuit of happiness are actions going on, then pursuit
and possession designate alternative comprehensions of
one continuously diversifying process wherein going-on
is the goal of going, the end which is its own means.

Herein lives the reason why the mind, being an organ
of survival, opposes imaginative continuation to actual
stoppages. It sets against the body's death its own immortality, against *Thisworld* of the body's struggles for
survival and its own anxieties over survival, a dualized
Otherworld where the stuff of experience is heavenly
delight (yet minus the body's ears to hear and eyes to
see) or else is hellish agony (yet minus the body's sensibilities of nerves and blood and bones.) In this *Otherworld*
awareness is its own ground, and pleasure and pain are
ineffable; or else both are grounded in an ineffable total
awareness for which the philosophic name is usually
"God."

19. Immortality, Suicide, and Survival

Another token of the Western mind's commitment to
the body's survival and of its revulsion against death is the
appraisal of suicide which signalizes certain cultures and
religions. This is a conspicuous differentia of the manifold

diverse Christianisms, those being, more than anything else, directed to nullifying the actuality of death; in their Roman Catholic expression they condemn as mortal sin to save the mother and sacrifice the child of a deadly childbirth, to choose euthanasia as against dying of a torturously killing illness, or to commit suicide. Yet suicides outnumber accidental deaths in traffic, in the killings of battle. They are more frequent among town-dwellers than country folk, men than women; and, of course, Protestants than Catholics.

Theologians have not yet resolved the paradox of the dogmas which ban suicide in *Thisworld,* and affirm the certainty of immortal life in an *Otherworld* which can be genuinely merited in *Thisworld* only by a mortification of the flesh even unto its death in *Thisworld.* It is as if the *Otherworld* of images, signs and symbols consequent upon certain disorienting *thisworldly* transactions were the stakes of a wager more likely lost than won; as if this *Otherworld* were the desperate last bet on a better future, against ongoing experience of misery, defeat, and frustration, tamed by discourse and rationalized by arguments.

Of the latter, Socates' reassuring illations in the *Phaedo* are typical. Believers more convinced of immortality need little or no argument about death's mortality. They use death as a means to living ends such as revenge on an enemy by haunting him, depriving him of "face;" as repristinating personal power, or as setting at naught coercive power and freeing self from its persecuting domination. Inso far forth their behaviors, but not their perceptions, are like those of unbelievers certain of mortality. Each manifests his own singularity of conscious response to experiences of shock, to inner explosive centrifugal pressures, to outer disfigurations of topography and topology, to confusions of direction and blockings of passage. Awareness, in this condition, is such as might arise in drivers lost on a road where traffic signals no longer have any determinate signification, where all signs and directions are ambiguous, so that traffic has become a blind, anarchic veering of vehicles blindly piling up on one another. The awareness of such a driver would have shifted from the articulation of perception to the inarticulation of feeling. He would have been stopped, and also have ceased to look and listen. Looking and listening would be the initiation of renewed movement. Stoppage without them would be the breakup and reversion of confluences of movement into diffluent tensions whose gradients could be a descent toward disintegration and death. Articulate consciousness—which is so much an eventuation wherein activity translates from blind response to stimulation into behavior directly or symbolically channelled by hearing and seeing—may well have arisen as a spontaneous variation upon such disintegrative confrontations, serving to reform their blind impacts into orchestrated confluences, to convert their reciprocal arrests into reciprocally releasing and easing movements. Such reformations and conversions appear to be the role of consciousness in relation to the organism whose organtensions it supervenes upon, and to the circumambience wherein it supervenes. It is the role of a liberator and facilitator of the energies of survival in situations where they make for arrest or extinction.

Since such situations are at once the soil and sustenance of consciousness, every phase of it prolongs their tensor qualities. Even the most euphoric is taut with a certain elemental imbalance and asymmetry, an ineffable chronic feeling of insecurity, not the same as regret that the moment passes, but a poignant positive malaise for which a recurrent word is "anxiety." Philosophers like Schopenhauer or Sartre, psychologists like Freud, theologians like Kierkegaard, take this chronic positive poignancy for the ground of their rationalizations and arguments, transposing its normality into the abnormal acuities of "original"—and other—"sin," for feelings of "worthlessness," "dependence," "guilt," or "agony." Their creeds and codes are diversely adverted toward the purging of this illth and toward salvation from its predestinate consequences. They have had their forerunners and have their successors. Save for a few Cyreniacs, Epicureans and Stoics, all have recognized death for the sure cleansing and saving event, but not death by suicide, not death as the annihilation of consciousness, only death as the assumption of consciousness from uneasiness to security, from sad poignancy to triumphant ecstasy.

Whether suicide can in fact be a conscious seeking of the annihilation of consciousness continues an open question. Unless it be possible to be consciously unconscious, feelingly anaesthetic, livingly dead, suicide must always be a flight, never a pursuit. And on the record, that which it is a flight from is, in every case of suicide, some singularity of blocking and arrest, some impasse, where vision is impotent to redirect action, and mounting anxiety signalizes the compounding of inner tensions while the outer channels for their ideo-motor discharge are blocked, and no alternatives are prehended. Wherever this becomes the human condition, liberation is usually sought in fainting, in natural or artificial sleep induced by means of drugs, alcohol, and other narcotics. These accomplish an extinction, but not an annihilation, of consciousness. The drugged sleeper wakes, and meanwhile his organism is freed for intraorganic reorientation and a new ideomotor stance.

Here is the consequential, positive meaning of security, always and everywhere. It means a condition of freedom *from,* a levelling of the hindrances and barriers to the propulsive becomings which freedom *of, to* or *for* signify.Although suicide destroys the *sine qua non* of repristination, there is to date no acceptable way of appraising it otherwise than still an affirmation of life, an act defying and resisting the arrest, recoil, and disorientation of the powers of the struggling self to go on struggling.

Whatever a suicide bets his life upon—property, health, honor, love, the loyalty of friends and comrades —his self-slaughter signalizes his commitment to the values he despairs of preserving. In what concerns his image of himself, he is the unique seat of these values: their meaning to him, his responsibility for them—however pooled with meanings to, responsibilities of, other selves—remain indefeasibly his, and mount or fall with his powers to maintain them. Even the time and manner of his death are functions of his commitment. But there are times when others, who purport to be likewise guardians of the values but do retain the power—and thus hold the right—of command for their conservation, can decide when and where and how he who has lost the power shall die in order that the values may live. It not infrequently happens that those others are corrupt, disloyal, unworthy of the values in the keeping of their power. Then, because the believer is, as Josiah Royce phrases it, "loyal to loyalty," he surrenders his conscience and his will—like Socrates refusing to flee and taking the hemlock as a lesser evil than the evil of repudiating his greater good. Knowing that he is being entrapped, betrayed, and defeated in the name of the very ideals whose realization is his commitment, alert to their nullification at the hands of his superiors, he feels his values undermined, but nevertheless obeys the destroyers. Once committed, his not to reason why, his but to do and die, althrough he understands and finds nauseous the wills that command this. His submission, maybe, in his vindication of his integrity to himself, and its basic intent is projected oftener by laughter than by tears. It is a self-inflicted *auto-da-fé,* not infrequent in military, sacerdotal, and other authoritarian establishments such as the Jesuit order, the Nazi and Communist parties. The only alternative vindication open to a person so committed is suicide; and those who choose suicide do this because they believe that they can thereby defeat the prostitution of their values without profaning the values.

A community's appraisal of such acts will vary from age to age, region to region, and with the cultures and ruling passions of the times and places. Their altering configurations will vindicate or condemn the self-slaughter. When approved, the words for them are *"supreme sacrifice," "martyrdom," "positive devotion," "love," loyalty," "idealism."* When condemned, the words are *"cowardice,"* criminal folly," "gang-loyalty," "fanaticism," "madness."* But to minds at the point of thus intending death, such appraisals have become irrelevancies. They in no way qualify the singularity of the suicidal act or its import for the actor who, by performing it, still affirms life and pursues liberty.

Taken together, the struggle to be, the struggle to be safe, and the struggle to be free are one struggle to go on struggling; and its diversifying predicates signalize its external relations rather than its inner processes. Should any struggler's struggle come to that "moment of truth" wherein intent extinguishes consciousness, this also vindicates the values and valors which are conscious existence.

20. Philosophical and Psychological Interpretations of Man

Look from the instant presence of any person to his surroundings; look at what goes on between the two. You see a many-dimensioned spatial figure, never quite still, that you can delineate as a front where orchestrating internal energies encounter and engage a un-unified multitudes from other such fronts, animate and inanimate. A living person is a field of such activities never ceasing unless stopped. His inner forces pulse together from intra-cellular transactions within the separate and distinct organic structures that are his body and from the inter-organic ones between nerves and muscles, heart and kidneys and bloodstream, lungs and liver and glands and brain. Their ongoing synergy makes up his life as an organism and diversifies into his consciousness. His feel of this psychosomatic teamwork is his sense of self. It is as single, as simple, as ineffable as white light, and like white light, it supervenes upon a union of multitudinous diversities—particles or waves—into which it can be separated beyond reunion. Most of his days, a man thinks of himself as an individual, an indefeasible unity. Yet all that we know consequentially about this unity establishes that the man is a manifold; that his individuality here and now is a union, not a unity; that it is not prior to its parts, growing and shedding them as a beast its fur or a bird its feathers; that it is subsequent, *e pluribus unum*, and that soon or late scientific ingenuity can arrange for any organ to live and grow in complete isolation from its fellows in the organism or can replace even vital ones with either alien others grown in other bodies or with inanimate constructions devised to perform the relevant animate functions.

The team play of the diverse organs it is which creates and maintains the organic wholeness of the living organization, and the ways are countless for some member of the team—be it a single cell or an entire organ or group of organs—to cease playing, either spontaneously or responsively. We account such defections as diseases of the body, as stresses or sicknesses of the mind, or as interchangeably both. It is no accident that wholeness has long been a synonym for health, and that some physicians of the mind, teachers, and others occupied in any sort of "cure of souls," conceive their goal as "an integrated personality" or else an "adjusted personality." When the "integration" is imagined as a sequence of prevailingly harmonious transactions with the environment, the environment having the forming, and the individual the conforming role, the personality is "adjusted." When the process is understood as first an orchestration of inner diversities to whose formation the environment then is conformed, the personality is said to be "integrated." The distinction can sometimes imply no differences; sometimes irreconcilable ones. But a whole and healthy personality would be neither "integrated" nor "adjusted"; it would be at once an ongoing self-orchestration, orchestrating its environment with itself.

Operationally, a person's struggle for self-preservation is his struggle to preserve against arrest and dispersion, the union of diversifications whereof his living self consists. His individuality is struggle against dividuation; it is his struggle as an ongoing "integration" - "adjustment" to keep whole his going-on. His freedom is the mobile actuality of this orchestrating wherein he saves himself only as he makes himself, growing up, growing old, compounding experiences into memories, compenetrating memories into habits and altering them into images, screening them into concepts and projecting any and all in the conserving transactions with the world around which we signalize as perception. As felt, his freedom is his consciousness thus moving from next to next through the sequence of days and works. Their sequential union makes up the all of his personal history, and from it both his autobiography and biography could be only selections conformed to some pattern preferred by the selector.

The expression "the human condition" first and last signifies these sequences in their order of succession, and not their compenetrated instancy.

Endeavors to understand and appraise this condition are embodied in a diversity of philosophies of mind and of psychologies. Some focus on the compenetrated instancy. This they hypostasize as immortal soul or eternal spirit, endowing it with inalterable faculties or powers whose operations produce the altering sequences of the personal history yet leave the person's "original nature" to the last unaffected, unchanged. Others focus on the stream of experience. They set up a "psychology without a soul" and labor by means of introspection's backward look to explore the flow of consciousness, to distinguish repetitions and variations, to reduce them to no further reducible elements they call "sensations" and with those to build up an image of the mind as an order of recurrences, all having, at their progressive levels of complication, the same hierarchial structure. Psychoanalysts and gestaltists have practiced upon this method of explanation and appraisal extensive variations intending contentious dynamics of mind and consciousness. They have abandoned "sensations" for different units of construction. Nevertheless, they employ essentially static orders and relationships in forming their systems. Although they make do without immortal "soul," they pay the body only incidental heed, referring to its parts analogically or only when they must, like Bishop Berkeley referring to the eye in his explanation of vision. Behaviorists, per contra, pridefully do without not alone an immortal soul, but also the mortal stream of consciousness. They consider nothing but the body and its parts interacting with the environment in modes of stimulus-response, and they use "mind" and "consciousness," when they do use these terms, in order to denote chains of necessary stimulus-response sequences whereof the elemental unit of construction is a Pavlovian reflex.

Most schools of psychology except the psychoanalytical tend to expound mind as a given structure of necessary present connections. I can recall none which purport to be "scientific" that present it as a compenetrated instancy of contingent formations. The former yields stronger feelings of certainty than the latter; it harmonizes more readily with the pretensions, if not with the successes, of the more reliably predictive sciences. Nevertheless, the schools on the whole give evidence of emphases shifting from standstill pattern to propulsive process, from necessary connection to developmental formations and statistical sequence. In fact, this trend might well be due to contagion from a disposition, communicating itself widely to every modern variety of the scientific enterprise, to regard a man as a succession of eventuations uniting into a measurable stretch of time; to conceive the succession as gathered, at any moment of it, into a given configuration of space; and concurrently to look upon the man's character, powers, and potentialities as a living past going on in a self-forming personal history. Some imaginative psychologists carry back this personal history to the formations which follow one another in the mother's womb, and even to those within the genes whose combining at conception are believed to initiate, or at least to give a new turn to, the biography-making action. Imaginative philosophies could look back upon the genes themselves as particular new turns of sequences continuing through the stretches of times before there were any genes.

Should these sages be bored or appalled by the infinitudes along which such regressions would take them, they could stop by inferring free initiations, unceasing spontaneities, without cause and without direction. They could signalize them as quanta spurting *ex nihilo*. They could imagine some uniting sequentially as they come along next to next and are at last enmassed into the physicist's waves and particles, and thereupon manifesting the behaviors which the latter's discourse of waves and particles postulates. Thence the philosophic imagination could envision the formations spending and restoring themselves; converging; diverging; interfusing; diffusing; they could picture the formation as at some intervals happening into multitudes of compenetrations and unions; they could think the latter as both lasting and diversifying yet not separating. Imagination and reflection could see them even gaining energy and stability in diversifying, ever more successfully compensating outgo by intake, repelling what would break up their union from without, excreting what they cannot assimilate and naturalize within. Thus, they could conclude, the configurative teamwork preserves itself not only, but heightens and grows and changes as it preserves itself.

A philosophic imagination could envision this process going on until its energies have spent themselves beyond restoration. A reasoner might decide its singularity to be a shaping-up of the manifold interplay of spontaneity and order, chance and law, repetition and variation, necessity and freedom. These words signify qualities which experience everywhere encounters and theories of evolution purport to account for. They intend ultimately the interplay of cosmos and chaos implicit in the findings of the sciences of nature as well as the feelings of men. The interplay is a sequence of eventuations; every event is a happening with a start and a finish; every one from start to finish coincidentally makes itself as it spends itself. For all living is also a process of dying—which intake delays and stretches out—resisting untimely termination by aggression from without or by exhaustion within. Organisms—with their diverse organs and their diversifying inner transactions and outer actions; with their sequences of development from birth to maturation to senescence and death; with their processes of sleep and waking, eating, loving, hating, fighting, working and playing—all taking different and altering forms among plants and animals and men—are growths from these roots.

21. Relations: Their Role in Being and Becoming

The formation of orders, organic or other, begins as chance associations and culminates as necessary or intentional connection. The initiating relations are contingent and external; the bonds of union are loose and easily part. They signalize only the event that existences different from one another are come together. Their togetherness is only aggregation, mass, mob. If it persists, it changes as it persists into an organization; the bonds uniting its members to one another become tougher, more tensile, more enduring, more susceptible of stretching and straining without breaking. The whole which ensues as they hold is still a whole which can perish without the coincident extinction of its parts; it is a bare configuration of parts; it cannot exist unless its parts exist while the parts can go on existing whether in the whole or not; the relations between them are still external. If and as they continue to endure, their operational character alters. The habituation of the parts to one another is a process changing the relations between them from externality to internality: their connections, beginning in contingency, climax into necessity. Their intensification works a configuration over into a figure, unifies an organization into an organism. The external relations between the parts are therewith consummated in the organic internality which we experience in living forms. The whole into which they unite the parts is now such that, except as active parts of that whole, the parts must perish; they now so belong together that none can survive deprived of its transactional bonds with its fellows in the whole, although the whole can keep going on deprived of some of its parts but not of certain ones such as heart or lungs or kidney or brain. This holding together is believed to manifest a maximal intensity in the nucleus of atoms, and Whitehead argued that atoms are organisms.

But if atoms are organisms, then what we usually call organisms are by comparison only organizations, for they may be much more readily separated into their parts, and the parts by human ingenuity enabled to live independent lives. To dissolve the union of parts making up an intra-atomic nucleus, on the other hand, calls for a solar explosion or a terrestrial tornado in a cyclotron or bevatron. But it is noted that if the components of a nucleus converge and cohere, they also generate divergences and repulsions. If outer impacts impel them to ever closer compenetrations and identifications, they also thrust apart in mounting momentums of disruption and explosion. The simplest as well as the most complex formation on the earth and in it, and in all the patterns of the heavens, evince these stresses of fate and fortune.

Traditionally, philosophic attention is directed to eliciting or creating an unchanging identity on which to ground and with which to consummate all such unions of diversities and diversifications. But it must be clear that neither pure experience, nor the sciences engaged in exploring, understanding, directing pure experience, provide an unambiguous basis for such ground. The lifespan of any existence is not an inalterable sameness, but an altering differentiation. Even if differentiations start in one and only one event, they do not continue so, nor is oneness their foregone conclusion. Oneness figures always and everywhere rather as a consummation devoutly wished; and occasionally as a union precariously achieved and maintained against ever-renewing disruptive pressures from without and centrifugal trends within.

This is the perception that Henry Adams transposed into the anxious image of his antithesis between the virgin and the dynamo and his brother Brooks into the depressed fiction of the degradation of the democratic dogma. This is what today's physicists project via their incommensurable first and second laws of thermo-dynamics. This is what one school of existentialist philosophers project when they appraise the human condition as an existence without God, without ground, and without goal, "condemned" to be free and predestined to death, while another such school appraises it as an agonizing soul's free act of faith, grounded in God and destined by God to be saved from this death. The latter might be said to translate the physicist's law of the conservation of energy into the images and dogmas of theological discourse, while the former translate the physicist's law of the dissipation of energy into a dialectic operating with phenomenological postulates. Both bespeak the torsive tensions of man's struggle to live and not die; the anxiety which consummates tension as awareness, and the perceptions, deliberations, and decisions whereby the tensions turn toward synergy and whereby reciprocal inhibitions, obstructions, and coercions transpose to the orchestrated facilitation which is the pursuit of liberty.

22. Force and Freedom in Man's Inhumanity to Man

If a specific configuration of flesh and blood and bone and consciousness actually perceiving, deliberating, choosing, deciding, is that which a free man is here and now known as, then what else can his freedom be? What else is there, but this total stretch of his personal history compenetrated to his present instancy? It is the end, at once attained and pursued, which his struggle to go on struggling intends. Nor can there be any means to it other than the single events of his personal history, like the phrases of an ongoing melody suffusing one another as they follow one another, until all, interpenetrated and orchestrated, are the instant total of immediate experience. In the order of their succession, the events are the pursuit of the liberty whereof the orchestral instancy is attainment and maintenance. Both as end and as means this liberty is the process of determinations which signalize a person's transactions with a diversifying outer manifold whose own part, active or passive, is commonly more to bar, obstruct, or oppose than to release, nourish, and facilitate that orchestrated going-on.

In these transactions, other human beings play continuously far more intimate and dramatic parts than non-human existences. They are, hence, far more passionately weighted and valued. To man, nature, however violent and deadly, signifies less than man. We read much less about humanity's struggle with nature than about man's struggle for survival with man. Tradition denotes the latter as the war of all against all. This war is somehow not appraised in the same way, nor by the same standard, as the human struggle in nature for survival and its survival as fit by natural selection. For the inhumanity of man to man, systems of supernaturalism provide special designations not applicable to the indifferences and violences of nature. The unconscious premise and foregone conclusion of them all is the experience which pervades every man's life: that he world he spends it in is not one that was made for him; that his living is an unremitting struggle to save himself from being made over by one or another of the world's denizens fighting to fit him to itself and thereby unfitting him for himself, while at the same time he works and fights to make as many over as he can to suit himself. Each, being an indefeasible individuality, renders each a "problem of evil" to the others. In consequence, freedom *for* any becomes tantamount to freedom *from* the loves, the crammings, the flatteries, as well as *from* the animosities, the demands, the vilifications, the aggressions, the degradations, the starvation, the enslavements, the slaughter and destruction of others. These words signalize attitudes and intentions more commonly than performances, and their motivation can be demanding love as readily as hate. They are pervasive, but not as visible drives, in much that is called "peaceful competition"; they develop a high visibility in wars both cold and hot.

Freedom *for* or *in* or *of* or *to*, or simply *freedom*, would appear to be primal and "absolute." It is rendered relative, and new secondary characteristics accrue to it, whenever another such absolute comes actively into its presence. For absolutes must by definition be eternally the same, unaltering within, inalterable from without. If a multitude, they must be immobile Leibnitzian monads shut away and cut off from all intercommunication, incapable of any transaction whatsover, inner or outer. If a sole, self-contained, and self-containing One Absolute, it must be a homogeneous substance, a subject which cannot be its own predicate, nor an effect of itself, since subject and predicate, effect and cause, are terms of relation and signify diversity, sequence and change or signify nothing at all. The freedom of an absolute, be it a total many or a one alone, can never be a freedom *from* anything, since it has no bonds to anything, and it cannot free itself from itself; nor can its freedom be a freedom *for* anything, since it is by definition sheer, ineffable, inalterable being from which alteration and becoming are utterly excluded. To predicate freedom of an absolute is, in fact, to predicate change of the changeless, relations of the unrelatable, contingency and chance of necessity, indetermination within the inalterably determinate. Such predications are made, usually by theologians, and are made of whatever any of them means by "God." They are also signalized as mysteries; but the time is still future when theological mystery can make philosophical sense.

If, then, freedom means anything whatsoever, it means sequences of differentiation, relationships alterative and altering. Once more, its import is of a verb, not a noun. It signalizes transactions wherein the most foregone conclusion is not wholly foregone, wherein no same ever returns as quite the same, no sum is ever only a numbering of its parts, no effect ever nothing but a consequence of its cause. The transactions which freedom signalizes are eventuations becoming events, attended with contingencies, beset with chances, and suffused with spontaneous variations that, even when coming harmoniously *with*, do not follow necessarily *from*, the successive spurts and patternings which flow together as the stream of experience.

If the experience of freedom in experience is authentic, experience comes to perception as a confluence wherein concurrently the past which "can't be changed" is being changed, and the future which is nothing at all is being created. "Self-preservation," "struggle for survival," "will to live," "freedom of the will," "will to believe," "choice," "decision," and other such expressions are diversely intended to signalize these goings-on.

Perhaps it is a deficiency of language as of all signification—a deficiency resisting all repair and beyond compensation—that it so persistently fails to denote the
uniqueness of that which it is denoting. This is the condition that the self is preserved only as it changes, that it
survives only as it dies and exists only as it passes; that
"the will" works as a sequence of by no means congruent
willings and exercises its freedom no less in submissions
conceded, conformations accepted, rules consented to,
than in liberties taken, or pursued or defended and
maintained. In this condition, moreover, this fact is
operative: that the power which a will submits, conforms,
or consents to, must needs itself be in itself and for itself
a pursuit of liberty, a struggle to keep going its own
uniqueness of repetition and variation.

23. Freedom *From* as Security, Security as Law

There are those who appraise the condition of mankind's togetherness as a predicament. If it be such, then
it is peoples' endeavors to free themselves from the predicament which brings mature civilization to attend more
variously to *freedom from* than to that intrinsic liberty
which, with life and the pursuit of happiness, is declared
to be an "unalienable right." Intrinsic liberty a living
man takes for granted, like the beat of his heart and the
breath of his nostrils, like those sequences of relationships
and transactions with air and water and all that dwell
therein which are nuclear to the man's living at all. But
the propulsions which are teamed up into *this* man and
no other, whose singular union constitutes *his* personal
pursuit of liberty, soon cross and hinder or bar other

such teamings up, familiar or strange. The ensuing delays, obstructions, confusions, disorder, and arrests are sometimes circumvented by the detours called taking thought or reflection, ultimately by breakthrough and the imposition of preponderant force. Soon or late, submission to the latter's dominance becomes habit in the individual, custom in the community, and in the consciousness becomes belief that this coercion signalizes an authentic right and not an arbitrary power. Whereupon the belief gets transmitted to the generations by a teaching and by a tradition which present it trans-valued into authority as divine revelation, without regard to the fact that the seat of the authority is not in the force which exercises it but in the acquiescence of the persons suffering it.

Freedom from expresses a recognition of this condition and signalizes the reciprocal removal of barriers interposed by any man to the pursuit of their liberties by all men. Hence that passionate but frustrated libertarian Immanuel Kant, who happens to be the favored initiator of the modern philosophical argument concerning the condition, iterated that "freedom is being independent from the coercion of another's will . . . the inborn quality of every man in virtue of which he ought to be his own master by right." Experience, however, discloses that each man can enjoy this right of ruling himself as he was born to do only as all men pool their powers of rule in such wise as would estop any from arbitrarily coercing any other. Such a pooling initiates what comes to be called "the government of laws, not men"; it endows men with "equal liberty under law."

Insofar as "law" signifies what it obviously must—authority suffusing preponderant force—it is constituted by the teamwork of free submission and regulated dominance. Governments, when operating as such a teamwork, are governments by consent, whatever be their field of rule—political, religious, economic, esthetic, scientific, gaming, and so on. All varieties then postulate a certain transaction between outer compulsion or necessity and inner freedom or contingency; they eventuate as the parties to the transaction who are doing willingly what has to get done, willy-nilly; as their united readiness to pursue liberty as they must. The liberty intrinsic to this transaction is an adaptive liberty.

If its synergy mounts, it diversifies in mounting; during the process the meanings of *equality* tend to get transposed from equalization—another word is "justice"—by the removal or atrophy of coercive power, to equalization by replacement and conversion of coerced powerlessness. The intent of "law" shifts from the regulation "an eye for an eye and a tooth for a tooth" to the requirement of replacing lost eyes and teeth with better ones, either at the cost of the depriver alone or of the entire community. Equality as *freedom from* is transformed into security as *freedom of* or *freedom for*. The liberty intrinsic to this transaction is an integrative liberty.

24. The Witness of the Philologist

Philological contexts of the word "free" and its Indo-Germanic cognates and derivatives would seem to support the foregoing observations. The contexts enmesh "free" with the Sanskrit root "pri," which is translated "please," and which diversifies into "priya," meaning "dear" or "cherished." "Free" is also allied with the Anglo-Saxon "freen," "freogan," signifying "to make love," and "freond," "the lover beloved." These words connect obviously enough with the Germanic "freund," and "befreunden," whose English equivalent are "friend" and "befriend." (This the dictionaries equate with "to serve affectionately," "to woo," "to court," "to make love to.") "Freund" diversifies readily enough into "freude" which is Englished by "joy"; and "freien," which we translate into "enjoy," "celebrate." A more literal translation would be "to behave freely," which goes well with "befreien," to liberate or set free. Less literal is the diversification into "frieden," meaning peace. "Fried" - "rich" is a prince of peace in a frith or firth, i.e.: a quiet enclosure of land or water not under pressure from any "feind," that is, from any "fiend" or "foe." The god of such a place of peace is Frey whose sun and rain bring plenty; its goddess is Freya or Frigga who presides over the love and friendship that breed the plenty.

The word "liberty" figures similarly in a network of verbal variants with diversifying meanings. The network interweaves it with "libido," "deliver," "lief," "love," "libation" and their cognates and derivatives. It unites "liberty" to Liber, the pre-Roman Italian divinity presiding over vineyards and wine, drink and drunkenness, whom the Romans assimilated to Bacchus. A "libation" is a pouring of wine upon the ground or over a sacrificial animal as a drink-offering to whatever god. Pouring, as an act of worship, seems to signify equally with that which is poured. It somehow releases "libido," sets desire toward fulfilment, in an impulsion that pleases. The word for pleases is "libet." It goes with the Sanskrit root, "lubh," which the Anglo-Saxons wrote "léof" and their descendants wrote "lief," and we moderns write as "love." To love is "to have liefer," or, as the Germans say, "liebhaben." To love is to be "liberal," that is, open-minded and open-hearted, generous and candid; naturally out-going, and living from one's own integrity uncompelled and unafraid. The philological context of "liberty," in sum, signalizes the "libidos" impelling the "liberal" and "lover," which please in and of themselves. Liberty postulates spontaneity and autonomy. Philosophers would seem to confirm the implications of philology. John Locke, for example, writes somewhere that liberty is ". . . the power [of] a man to do or forbear doing any particular action according as its doing or forbearing has the actual preference in the mind." This is natural to the human condition, and its being natural Locke defines as man's being "free from any superior power on earth and not under the will or legislative authority of man, but to have the law of nature for his rule." Apprehended Lockewise—and Locke initiates a gradient of which Kant is a step—liberty is neither a privilege nor a right due to a grant from a power that can freely give or withhold. On the contrary, it is the original pouring-forth, the ongo-ing nativity of intention, deliberation, decision, and propul-sion which grows up and grows old as it keeps "aborning."

The analogies are patent between these significations and the mutating meanings of "freedom" and "liberty" which the dictionaries count up. The condition which Kant signalizes even more than Locke appears to be focal. In relation to his environments, natural and human, a free man is first and last *free from* their hindrances and coercions; he is a man let alone, let be, let do, (*laisser faire*), spared their interference, and insofar as thus spared, a man favored and loved, his mobility and self-direction unchecked, his goings-on unimpeded, his roads all unbarred, open without price, gratuitous like divine grace. In himself and of himself the man is the friendly, loving, liberal spirit, the generous heart and will, whose own pursuit of liberty nourishes and supports the same pursuit by others, interposing itself against arrest by necessity or obstruction by chance. When many so join together their several freedoms as by means of this union of personal powers to institute equal security for the freedom of each from subjection to any, custom calls the ensuing condition liberty. It is the "liberty under law" which the institutions of democratic societies are so hopefully devised to serve and nourish. Democratic pronouncements stress that the institutions are means, not ends; and that their first rôle is to be ever vigilant against arbitrary encroachments upon the primal freedom which each man discloses as his personal history going on, but also encloses as a unitary person present here and now. Democratic institutions serve, secondly, as means enabling every man to diversify and enhance this freedom of struggle to go on struggling in a progressive abundance of ways and works.

25. Intellect and Intelligence as Freedom Pursued; Freedom As Knowledge

If the institutions, arts, and sciences of civilization receive from history more than incidental meaning, the more which endures is the liberation of individuality just signalized. Their values, as the works of man for the hearts of men where alone values can have any seat, live in this multiplication and heightening by which freedom consciously progresses as at once going and goal.

Now insofar as the progression is self-aware, the

pursuit of liberty is the pursuit of knowledge by means of knowledge. This is the vital spring of the unyielding ages-old faith that reason is the uniquely human formation of power. For reason consists in part of the intelligence which orchestrates to one another diverse existences, ends and means; it consists of the arts of consensus; and in part reason consists of the intellect which operates as a configuration of semantic procedures with images, symbols, signs, and their relations; which is their manipulation in discourse as surrogates for persons, places, and events. Reason is the reciprocal suffusion of intelligence or workmanship, and intellect, or wordmanship and—not merely an occasion—swordsmanship or the strategy, tactics and logistic of the arts of war.

But wordmen, such as theologians and philosophers, are traditionally disposed to isolate reason to intellection, and to hypostatize the power of the word as the instant master of all becoming: "In the beginning was the Word, and the Word was with God, and the Word was God . . . And the Word became flesh and dwelt among us full of grace and truth."

Workmen, such as herdsmen and farmers and carpenters and smiths and masons and weavers and painters and potters, are traditionally men whose vital words are books of recipes and of rules for making and producing. Their consciousness is rarely discursive, regularly perceptive, and is often called "intuitive." Its existence is the feel of the sequences of production ensuing upon the dynamic give-and-take between stuffs and tools whose *terminus a quo* is one thing and whose *terminus ad quem* is quite a different thing. Their intelligence is the manipulative skill channelling memories and perceptions which project the product and control the process; it is workmanship—knowledge *in actu*, knowhow. It is power over nature and in society: the singularity of every enduring culture lives in and from it.

When the skills of the word and the skills of the work are permitted to become confluently functions of one another, this union of discourse and manipulation consummates in an orchestration of intellect with intelligence for which today's most expressive symbol is "science." Science brings the power of the word and the power of the work to an optimal synergy. More than any other form of knowledge, science is Francis Bacon's knowledge which is power—power over nature in knowledge of nature, power in man and over man in knowledge of mankind—and science in and of itself is thus man's most efficacious vehicle of his pursuit of liberty.

Altogether, mankind's struggle to go on struggling is its struggle to extend and diversify the knowledge wherewith it can freely pass beyond the barriers set by space, by time, by things and by thoughts, by their necessary connections and by the chances and changes which attend them. Human freedom maintains itself and enlarges not alone as it resists these compulsions and these intrusions, but also as the men purposefully pursuing their freedom learn to alter its relations to necessity and contingency from those of passive subject to those of active ruler. Till now the method of science has been at once the most promising learning and the most reliable practice of this alteration. Till now it works more hopefully than any other formation of mankind's pursuit of liberty to maintain and enlarge its ongoing *élan* vis-à-vis the compulsions of fate and the contingencies of fortune, and to harness both to the service of this struggle to go on struggling which is man's life.

As the current formulations of the sciences of nature present fate and fortune, the latter's primal manifestations are chaos—the indeterminate initiations of events, their random impacts, combinings and separatings, some of which slowly and chancefully compound into the stable configurations we call cosmos. These configurations manifest "law and order" and are thereby "rational." They go on in recurrences and cycles whose parts appear to follow one another thus and only thus and never otherwise. Their connection is hence appraised as necessary, and the order of their succession as a causal sequence. To scientists such an order exemplifies "determinism" or "mechanism"; to humanists it stretches out the inescapable hand of fate. But the perspectives of the modern point of view render determinism, mechanism, and fate passing eventuations amid what may, by a somewhat forced metaphor, be called an environment of indeterminism, diversity, and fortune. The sequent repetitions are formations arising in this environment when components of it distinguish themselves within it by coming together in such wise that each holds and redirects the propulsions of the other to a reciprocity with its own, and the reciprocities compound with others into an orchestration which "music of the spheres" so imaginatively suggests. The term "environment" is metaphorical because the orchestration does not annihilate their original relationships either observationally or logically. Initiations and terminations keep occurring within their union; change and chance continue to qualify and divert its mechanisms and necessities. Cosmos' vital centre is chaos still; the life of necessity is freedom.

26. Human Freedom vis-a-vis Fate, Fortune, and Death

Man has been called a "microcosm," a little cosmos. And theological vanity and natural self-flattery aside, man is such. For, as of the record, his human organization and history as pursuit of liberty manifest and project their own singular orchestrations of original liberty and natural necessity. We may understand human nature as a unique harmonization of fate and fortune amid an uncontrollable aggregate of like uniquenesses; we may recognize human freedom as the human struggle to keep up and enlarge its own uniqueness both by inhibiting and nullifying disruptive inner variations of body or mind, and liberating, and orchestrating with, confirmatory ones. Of course, neither is an eventuation inside the skin alone. Of course, wherever consciousness is present and mind is *in action*, both are sequences either concurrent with or ensuing upon ongoing psychosomatic transactions with surroundings made up of not less singular interplays of fate and fortune. From the point of view of the sciences of man, the sequence is the formation of character and the making of personal history.

Schools of historians record this pursuit diversely, according to the passions and desires which project their faiths and order their value-systems. But what record does not signalize a sequence of changes whose uniquenesses it ignores, perhaps, but which it cannot and does not reduce to futures disclosing repeated identicals and nothing else? Considering how history makes itself and how historians write it, the maxim that history repeats itself is one more projection of a wish, not the observation of a happening. That which only repeats itself is not history, and that which history is does not repeat itself, be it the life-story of an individual or of any association of individuals, be it ephemeral or lasting. From his own stance among neighbors and strangers, amid the symbols and structures signalizing the works of man, and amid the goings-on of his non-human surroundings, each man, as he struggles to keep on struggling, creates and enacts his own rôle in a play of which his rôle renders him part author. He makes and remakes himself as he lives along; and his personal destiny other than death is no foregone conclusion that a social scientist can draw or an historian prophesy. The man's individuality, from birth to death, is indefeasible, and its road as the pursuit of liberty which is his living-on, is ineffably singular. He creates it as he ages, moving upon his originating propulsions into the habits that team up as his character. The spontaneities that keep suffusing and altering the habits yet orchestrate with them into this personal history, so that the last day of his life comes as unpredictable diversification from its first day.

Although what any single individuality evinces need not qualify any whole consequent to the coming together of single individuals—indeed, have not metaphysicians and theologians and others proved that "Man" goes on forever while men only come and go?—there is still nothing in the configuration of any known society which could provide a scientific tip to bet on the metaphysical and theological likelihood the whole won't end up as its parts end up. Few contend that the race of men, the diverse societies into which its members associate, do not soon or late become as extinct as the members. Insofar as there is a destiny, death is that destiny. But before death, goes the living of life, and societies and individuals may alike shape their struggles as a fear of death or as a zest for life. The former may be said to live dying; the latter, to die living. Either way, man ends, or ends as man while struggling to stay man, even as the ancestral ape ended as ape while struggling to stay ape.

True, man's utter ending, his complete extinction, is a necessary conclusion even as it was a necessary conclusion for other species, from whose dead vestiges we rebuild imaginary organisms struggling to keep themselves alive. Nor is it excluded that man's extinction might be so complete as to leave not a rack behind. Nevertheless, insofar as the struggle to go on struggling is the life-giving spring of the philosophic tradition, philosophy recoils from utter annihilation. If the speculative imagination cannot vindicate a *de facto* personal immortality, with its living past and conscious remembering and intending, it devises with Plato a dead and forgotten past with unconscious remembering and intending; or it blows up an impersonal present consciousness with Aristotle, or one of imperishable present pastness with Spinoza, or an eternal recurrence with Nietzsche, or a sequence of consciousness discontinuously continuous with Leibnitz, or Fechner, or even William James in the West, and with the karma-fearing eschatologists of the East. Goethe's rhyme points up the inveterate propensity:

> *Nichts vom Vergänglichen*
> *Wie's auch geschah*
> *Uns zu verewigen*
> *Sind wir ja da.*

All those inventions of the philosophers, to say nothing of the hypostases of the theologians, look to some sort of termination of the struggle to go on struggling which yet should be no termination of the consciousness which is the struggle's expression, or the mind which is its agent and instrument. The philosophers and theologians intend consciousness to go on in delight and at peace; if it cannot eternally, as some realize, then from everlasting unto everlasting, with nothing to learn, nothing to forget, everything the same. Such intentions usually devalue knowledge as the pursuit of liberty, and thus as an unceasing learning and forgetting, acquiring and discarding, such as the sciences practice and the arts express. Christian doctrine, indeed, elaborating on the Eden story, attributes the pursuit of knowledge to a fall from grace, equates sinfulness with knowledge, innocence with ignorance, ignorance with bliss, wisdom with folly. Churchmen who are the doctrine's custodians and chief beneficiaries have been among the earliest and most persistent in endeavors to police and bring to a standstill the pursuit of knowledge which is the pursuit of liberty. Their communist, fascist, nazi and communazi competitors in infallibility, each postulating salvation on a rival body of doctrine equally or even more antipathetic to the freedom of the mind, follow a similar policy. Each sets up his own kind of barrier against alternatives. Each inhibits inquiry and discussion, licenses publication, maintains an *index expurgatorius*, censors literature and the arts, sentences disobedience and punishes variation as a sin against God or treason against the state. But none pays any attention to the event that immuring men's struggle to go on struggling within these keeps of body and mind does not end its processes; that the immuration only imposes on them a different direction and form. The wardens and keepers intend both of these to be circular. They bet their authoritarian security on recurrence without variation; and the consequences to the human spirit, of their devices to make their bet a wager on a sure thing, is a starved repetition and elaboration of creeds, and a caged rehearsal of codes, unfitting it for transactions with an environment which keeps altering form and direction alike.

On the record it is by those transactions, as they multiply and diversify, that the humanity of man grows into strength and freedom; it is by their means that humanity vindicates the singularities of its freedom against the interpositions of fortune and the impositions of fate. As Francis Bacon had pointed out in his *Advancement of Learning*: "To say that a blind custom of obedience should be a surer obligation than duty taught and understood, is to affirm that a blind man may tread by a surer guide than a seeing man can by a light." We might further say, indeed, that the pursuit of liberty through this pursuit of knowledge is the pursuit of light, and by light for light.

2

The Actual and the Ideal in the Pursuit of Liberty

THE ACTUAL AND THE IDEAL
IN THE PURSUIT OF LIBERTY

1. Freedom: The Substance and the Shadow

Our experiences of actual freedom come as experiences of futurity. We realize them as pulses of duration with varying spans. Even perceiving the past is such an impulsion forward, a thrust and flow *beyond*. The word "beyond" signalizes a new *now*, the present coming of a *soon*. We perceive it as an awareness beating forward, pulsing untrammeled or pushing against obstruction and delay. The successive beats, be their intent remembrance or anticipation or apprehension, shape up a pattern which forms as they compound and which delineates the beats while consummating their interpenetration. We experience futurity wherever attention shifts from *was* or *is* to *might be* or *about-to-be*, from *here* to *beyond*. The shift is the frontier between the two, where determinate *now* diversifies into determining an undetermined *next*. Futurity comes as a heightened sense of an ongoing transit to something insecure and uncertain, from something safer and surer. The shift of attention is an act of faith. It is a choice and a decision. The chooser bets that some past will somehow go on as present, that remembrance will repeat as recognition, that anticipation will mount into fulfillment. His bet is, however, an open bet; it takes a chance. Hedge as he may, there is no foregone conclusion that he will win. The chances and changes intrinsic to freedom exclude the foregone conclusion; the bets that are postulated on it cannot be guaranteed bets on a sure thing.

The ideal of guarantee, immediate or ultimate, is a compensation for, not a confirmation by, our experiences of actual freedom.* The ideal is the substance of things hoped-for, imagination's impatterning of desire. In any personal history, it is the shadow of fulfillment which desire unfulfilled calls up from remembrance. In none does this shadow ever transubstantiate into the real presence of fulfillment. Fulfillment is either a slowed-up transit going-on, or it is a terminal stoppage. The slow-ups, like the meals we eat, come as different or smoother, slower, more deliberate propulsions still directed future-ward; they continue and confirm freedom. A stoppage or termination finishes freedom; it is the death of that freedom. The mobilities of change and chance collapse into immobility and stasis. But according to certain ideal-ists, immobility and stasis nevertheless continue the mobility, and forever. They define the collapse as termina-tion but without cessation, as culmination going on although culminated, as consummation at once consum-mated and yet consummating. Often, they proclaim that this exhaustion of freedom into process which does not proceed, into event with no eventuation, is the true freedom, the higher, sole, ontological freedom which only an eternal with no beyond possesses, or some monistic god incarnates. Obviously the paradox is a flight from the freedoms we live *as* and *in* and *by* and *for*. Those freedoms are ever movements *beyond*, pursuits with their faster and slower tempos, but not arrests or terminations.

---

* This is one reason why Christian theologians give divine grace so paramount a rôle in their drama of salvation, which Dante signalizes as the Divine Comedy.

They do not collapse into one unaltering pursuit of its own unalterable self, or into a self-repetition which does not repeat but so mirrors itself in itself that image and original are not two but one and the same. Actual freedom is alteration, innovation unforeseeably going on, stretching instancy into process, enlarging, exalting the eternal into the temporal.

It is the philosophies of the great tradition that do thus transvalue termination and pursuit. The "perennial philosophy" is a many-tongued argument to the effect that this ideal alone is the actual, that the actuals we experience are illusion. According to most of its spokesmen, the heart cannot feel secure nor the mind certain save where they prehend changelessness as both the ground and goal of change, necessity or providence as the assurance of freedom. They argue that the reliable can be only the inalterable; the instant only the eternal; that hence time and the future cannot be real. For what else except this alone which is always and everywhere one and the same can save us from the adversities of diversification, insure us against its uncertainties and insecurities, preserve us unwounded from its catastrophes and whole amid its disasters?

That their dialectical presentations of this supreme eternal and universal surety for our safety and freedom are themselves events, processes of transformation, redefinition, and reappraisal, the spokesmen of the *phillosophia perennis* usually ignore. They pretend it doesn't matter that their analyses and syntheses, their arguments of the foregone conclusion occur as beats of time with sequences from earlier to later (or premise to conclusion) which the earlier's struggles for its own survival bring to pass; they pretend that no one need mind that those, too, are struggles to go on struggling whose cessation is extinction. West and East, the philosophic tradition continues to carry forward diverse undertakings of the yearning heart and discursive head to demonstrate a struggler whose consciousness is self-consciousness only, and whose self-hood is happiness uncontaminated by any pain, and unstrained by any struggle. This consciousness they call "spirit," alive without aging, creative without effort, free without futurity, mind-stuff all power and knowledge and bliss, consummated in the unity which Hindus signalize as *satchitananda*. The recurrent commoner symbols for this one are such words as "God," "Allah," "Atman," "Brahma," "deity." Each stands for a number of diversifications of the idea of an eternal and universal consciousness conscious only of itself, unmoving yet the all-mover, changeless yet free, all-possessing, all-comprehending, yet excluding the times, the places, the evils, the agonies, the insecurities and uncertainties which are so largely the stuffs of every human career. The perenniality, the tradition, composes itself of these diversifications. Each of them comes as a traditionalist's replacement of an earlier by a later *philosophia perennis*, which he bets on as more certain to provide the final goal of an ever-renewing pursuit of safety and freedom. Each is a device whose deviser is striving that his own existence shall pass from the circumambience of his own culture to some such universal end-without-end.

2. Freedom as the Making and Working of Ideals

In view of their relation to the actual, these ends-without-end are called ideals. As recorded, they are ideas isolated, hypostatized, and attributed the power which has been used up in forming them, but the power heightened beyond calculation. By first intention, "idea," in its Greek or Latin or Sanskrit original, meant a seeing, a perceiving, a witting, a visioning. In due course it came to mean one such an experience preferred, a choice which therefore the chooser clung to, delayed in its passage, held back and caused to lag from fading into the past and from the mind's forgetting. By so doing, the chooser projects it toward the open, unexperienced future; he now uses it so to shape whatever might, or is-about-to-be as to assuage the heart's desire. That which does the shaping—the substance of the ideal—is the stuff of memory, signified by images and ikons and words, developed by argument, and chosen or ordained as rule. Perennial philosophies are those choices or ordinations impatterned in logical order. A later word for them is "ideology." They flow diversely from the common spring of all human endeavor—the ongoing transvaluation of the actualities of our struggle to go on struggling into an ideal of survival as a victorious struggle to put an end to all struggle and stay alive nevertheless.

Sometimes this aspiration is ascribed to the modes of restoring organic balance for which current usage, we recall, has accepted the word "homeostasis." Consciousness of such organic balance is said to be our innermost first experience of wellbeing; it is the consciousness of the foetus growing in the mother's womb. The place of growth is appraised as a world happily prepared for its guest, automatically suited to nourish its formation and support its behaviors. Foetal awareness is said to be all complacent feeling; its rôle nowise adjustment, alteration, but mounting enjoyment of the foetal state of grace.

By consequence, birth is as the Platonic myth suggests, truly a fall yet not a forgetting. Certain schools of thought, transposing Plato's, argue that all a person's living, and at last his dying, consists of a quest after that primal bliss, impelled by remembrance, led on by anticipation, and frustrated by actuality. The pursuit of happiness is thence the pursuit of the intra-uterine consciousness, an endeavor after its repetition and return. Living, these schools indicate, does reshape remembrance and bring apprehension, but neither alters its tone and timbre, nor modifies the primal images and formulae of anticipation. Such words as "heaven," "paradise," "nirvana," "utopia" express life's pain-apprehensive diversifications of the intra-uterine original. They also signalize the ideals, the materials, the tools, and the methods whereby the unforgotten, now unconscious, primal awareness is transvalued if not transformed. It is *terminus a quo* and *terminus ad quem* of diversifying psychologies, of arts of healing, and of philosophies of culture and civilization, with their contrasted appraisals of love, laughter, and tears. It is why tradition predominantly sets mankind's golden age in the past.

Yet, what is known regarding the actualities of intra-uterine existence can hardly be harmonized with this ideal of a godlike foetal consciousness. From conception to birth, foetal existence is a chain of change, ever inwardly off balance, never in stable adjustment with the outward uterine environment. Foetal relations to the latter make up a sequence of ongoing transactions between the foetus and a configuration of the womb's altering strains and tensions. The foetus' increase in weight, its sequential formation, its pushing, pressing, kicking movements, finally reach a span too large and too painful for its hostess. Parturition at last sets the mother free from the penalties of pregnancy via the pains and pangs of bringing forth. Birth is thus a dual liberation; for the newborn a kind of bursting of bonds become too tight and constrictive. There are those who speak of "birth-trauma" and who take the experience of being born as the matrix shaping character and development outside the mother's womb.

And if the womb, appraised as the fittest environment which a human ever experiences, is seen in fact to be so increasingly unfit, how much the more so must be the enviroment it is born into? There, the harmonies which the newborn attains are endlessly more precarious, its transactions with its surroundings are ever more unbalanced and transitional. Its existence presents itself more than ever as a struggle to go on struggling; its growth presents itself as a self-compounding of the struggle with its hopes and fears, its advances and retreats, its laughter and tears. And that which it is said to struggle for is a state of balance, an actuality of repose experienced, whose *de facto* attainment would be not survival but extinction. That which the actuality does consummate in is the spiraling sequence of feelings and strivings and doings which the word *homeostasis* can signify only in part. For at bottom *homeostasis* intends the unaltered recovery of a previous equilibrium, it means recurrence without change. But no personal history discloses such recurrence. The balance passingly restored consummates a series of transactions which have altered at its heart the balance lost, remembered and ostensibly sought. Such words as "hunger," "lust," "need," "want," "drive," "instinct," "impulse," "aspiration," "wish," "will," "interest" do signify either the feel of imbalance or the remembrance of balance-supplying objects or both compenetrated. Their content then is not alone their inner propulsion but also their satisfying pause and poise whenever propulsion gets shaped to quieter flow; whenever passion impatterns in vision, and turmoil subsides toward tranquillity. The shaping energies are signified by such words as "food," "friendship," "love," "sharing," "healing," "dress," "shelter," "war," "peace." Forms of sport, works of art, science, and religion include the more noticeable tranquilizing formations—we signalize them as "satisfactions," full-makings—brought to birth by the struggle for existence which changes as its transactions continue and continue only as they fail, and must fail if they are to continue.

3. The Role of Ideals: I. Imaginary for Perceptual Evil

This compenetration of continuation and lapse is accounted for in many ways, an ultimate one being the physicists' second law of thermodynamics; another such is the "death-instinct" of the Freudian sect of psycho-analysts. But in man's experience it is sufficient that no hunger is ever lastingly assuaged, that no food of flesh or spirit satisfies once and for all, nor is any provided that suffices for all mankind. Whatever be the economy—material, cultural, moral, intellectual—its mark is scarcity. Within any, the personal struggle to survive is a warfare between too many and too mighty demands upon too small a supply. There are, however, interludes when their homeostatic circling changes to spiral; its sequences then enter into new relationships upon new directions; conflicting demands pool their energies into a co-operative endeavor to replace unsharable scarcity by sharable abundance.

Like the competition of which they are a mutant, such endeavors fail whenever the workers and fighters are by nature themselves too weak to actualize the ideal which their weakness projects; too weak, that is, to achieve the task they set themselves. Then, like infants incapable of doing for themselves, they perish, no matter how great the abundance which surrounds them. They are too faint in body, too deficient in mind to reach or grasp the satisfactions they crave, even though the goods are to be had for the taking. Many weaknesses are inborn: Hand or heart or head or all together are by nature unable to cope. Many other weaknesses, perhaps many more than the inborn, are acquired or imposed.* Survival calls for enduring or surmounting both and, as struggle to go on struggling, is directed toward surmounting both. Pooling individual weaknesses to make collective strength happens as one way; another becomes supplementing them with outer support and building them to sufficiency by inner reconstruction. Tools and weapons develop as such supplements; rank, prestige and display, office and its insignia come to serve as such supports; education and the practice which makes perfect get established as such sufficers.

Often, when neither support nor sufficer can serve, a person or a people will balance with *fancied* powers and possessions the imbalance not to be overcome by actual ones. An idea of a world beyond nature gets built up to bring to equipoise the imbalance due to nature's thwart-

---

* Some traditions qualify inborn ones as original sin in man, acquired or imposed ones as ultimate evil in nature.

ings and obstructions. The economy of this supernatural compensates for and offsets the deficiencies of the natural. When the homeostatic force, of which the compensating ideal is the corrective phase, swings, as it often does, beyond the closure it would revert to, this imaginative excess heightens, instead of redresses, the imbalance it is supposed to bring back to balance. "Contrition," "grace," "salvation" name ideals which figure in such swings.

Laughter and tears, though apt to every economy, are often conspicuous in this one. For this one pushes beyond the movement which it is believed to culminate. The culmination is the envisioned terminal "good," wherewith we signify that termination without cessation, that unmoved and unmoving mobile whereinto we hypostatize some occasionally stable and harmonious economy of satisfactions, some interlude of good hap among the happenings of experience. Hypostasis transposes passage into arrival, relation into absoluteness, actual process into philosophical substance. Plato and all his epigons so transpose "good," and we have seen how, and with what disregard of their dialectic, imbalance and asymmetry continually undo this philosophical doing.

If mobility be "evil," then evil is inseparable from good and participates in its essence. What else are well-being, strength, or excellence of mind or of body, than activities taking place and going on? Smooth or turbulent, what do they signify, if not transactions with multitudinous surroundings, each a dynamic system willy-nilly taken up with its own upkeep and willy-nilly engaged with others' only as those bear on its own? However we may transvalue experience into ideals and rework the actual into the "real" of our safety and happiness, that which we so make over enters our lives and takes hold of our awareness as a procession of events not made for us and not caring whether we survive or perish. The weather of existence remains weather alike as the fluxes of nature and as the tides of human passion and action. We live on struggling with drouths and floods, earthquakes and wind-storms and tidal waves far more poignantly than we live seeking and savoring sky and sea, rain and earth and the fruits thereof. We live on struggling with bacilli and viruses, the spirochete, the gonococcus, the plasmodium, and the endlessly other infinitesmal invisible organisms which, innocently engaged on their own survival, convert the body and psyche of man into a laboratory of tortures, a theatre of disease and pain and sufferings which strike with unspeakable poignancy. We live on, struggling with spontaneous inward imbalances—deficiencies of glands, malignant excesses of cell-growths, conflicts of heart and head expressed as diverse hysterias, neuroses and psychoses with hurts whose cruelty no healthy imagination can picture.

We live on, again, struggling with one another, on every level of violence—from the violence of a war of words to the violence of war with weapons, all with their agonies and laughters and tears, pursuing each other's enslavement or extermination. Enslavement is a domestication of other men, similar to the domestication of plants and animals, compelling them to the victor's uses and converting them into the tools and materials of his satisfactions. Its limitations are of record, and one direction of the human pursuit of liberty is men's struggle to free themselves from their degradation into other men's tools with life in them, the cowed unwilling means to other men's ends. In the eyes of those whose ends are served, the means are works of providence, made for those ends, wherein all good is consummated. But to the consciousness of the vanquished and enslaved, is such a good, ordering such a world, the acme of an unseen, unsearchable but infallible cosmic benevolence? Is it the tool of a self-evident cosmic malice? Or are benevolence and malice both ideals, rationalizations or justifications of accidents of fortune, wherewith desire and need transvalue the contingent into the foreordained? Until consciousness and idealization hypostatize chance comings and goings into predestined means to eternal ends, are not victors and victims alike, innocent strugglers for their own survival, even as bacilli and viruses?

4. The Role of Ideals: II. The Humanization of the non-Human and the Domination of the Human

Whichever alternative be chosen, man's title to what ever he takes to be a means to his own survival, a servant of his good, is at least suspect. In the indifferent fluxes of nature, events come, go, and pass into and out of relations with one another which are good or evil by their rôle in each other's survival, while the title to survival stays unmodified whatever the rôle.

This is not the case with the power to survive: rôle may diminish or heighten power. And to the degree that warfare stays innocent, it consists simply in the pursuit of one's own liberty without intending the extinction of another's. Insofar forth the battles are fair and honorable. The destruction they bring is like that of the catastrophes of nature, without malignancy. It is such as Krishna advises Arjuna to emulate. Those struggles eventuate in an art and a wisdom that human enterprise carries from incantation to science, from ceremonial and rite to technics and engineering. The record of this carriage underlies the humanist "great tradition," which intends an ongoing humanization of the non-human. It is the source-material of every reliable history of civilization. Let be what they may the systems of belief wherewith companies of *genus homo* shape their ways and works into their singular configurations of culture. Every variable of them arises and develops as some human being's invention to bring aliency to intimacy, dependence to independence and independence to interdependence. Each is a device to transvalue the land, the waters, the tops and depths of both and all that dwell there from an indifferent or inimical co-existent into a friendly natural resource. Or it is a device to reconvert the natural resource, when it has in its turn duly become a challenge to survival, into a helper and nourisher. Each is a formation in a succession of formations which alter as they pass, playing their parts in the unceasing struggle of passions, persons, and peoples which each struggler innocently exacts from all by its struggles for its own freedom to live out its life. The valuations, the laughter, and the tears which distinguish moments in the career of such formations figure as appraisals of them, proper or improper. Laughter, like love, is exalted to divinity; and festivals celebrating the god of laughter become as signal religious events as festivals celebrating Dionysus or Diana of the Ephesian. They become matrices of the arts and ways for the pursuit of liberty.

So also are all prescriptions of propriety and ordinations of impropriety (whatever be the mode of the human enterprise they enclose), formations in idea to over- or by-pass barriers against the pursuit of liberty. But those which are neither man-made nor man-intended do not receive so much space in the record. Religion, literature, the dramatic and graphic arts concern themselves chiefly with man's thwartings of man. Tragedy drawing tears, and comedy drawing laughter serve both to appraise and to free from the thwartings. Some observers suggest that social institutions are more networks of such thwartings that linked highways of liberation, that they cannot be the latter. In peace or at war, the observers say, men are tethered and confined with one another, through traditions, customs, creeds, and codes; these dam up men's impulses, dampen and stop short their action; they impound men's indefeasible differences into reciprocal checks and challenges, so that even a fight to the death takes a form where each unequally constrains the freedom of the other. Mere numerical diversity of the otherwise identical—no less than essential differences which distinguish human beings from one another—contest as blocks and barriers through which passage must somehow be won. Physique, temperament, character, intelligence, native and nurtured, name, each, manifold interplaying propulsions strong and weak, able and deficient. Working upon the outer closures to passage and fulfilment, they shape up a changing pattern of the continuing transactions whereof our struggle for our existence consists. This, a variety of homeostatis, spirals from stability through instability to a new and reordered stability, different from before in matter and mode. The ideals which the workings strive to incarnate seek to dominate diversity when applied to other humans, and to subdue to human uses and assimilate to human forms when applied to the non-human.

5. The Role of Ideals: III. As Ends, as Means, and as Measures

Among our words for this spiralling are "growth," "development," "progress." These signify processes wherein identity maintains itself only as it alters, and alters as a continual conversion of the different into the same which is at once a differentiation of the same. Identity, too, is a verb, not a noun; it denotes a transaction both sustained and pursued by parties consisting of singular or collective individuals and of their enviroments. Identity is not reducible to the passing shape only of a present condition; it is experienced as a design for living not so much now, as with the time that comes. Futurity is of its essence. Thus, personal or collective identity is more ideal than fact, more standard of living aspired to than the actual events it inspirits. Its nucleus is a standard of survival, projected rather than attained, wherewith man the measurer, measures all things—those that are, that they are, and those that are not, that they are not.

As formations completing or compensating some deficient wisdom of the body, ideals, especially when they signalize the wisdom of the mind at points in a personal history where this diverges sharply from the wisdom of the body, are then mankind's measures of man, of his world, and of his destiny. As conscious intentions, they shape up into the plans and rules of life which creeds and their related codes embody. Ideals define a man's nature and goals to himself, and set the commonplace immediacy of his perceptions in translumining and transvaluing perspectives of which a striking example is the idealization of the tasteless vapid wafer of the Christian's communion by the dogma of transubstantiation.

Defining "to have," ideals measure the gap between it and "to have not"; at the same time they map the ways and designate the works which might close the gap and consummate fast in feast, scarcity in abundance, need and want in satisfaction, going in goal.

The antonyms just listed explicate the great tradition's polarization of goods and evils and ends and means. Implicit is the persistent sentiment that evil can be, and often is, a necessary means to good, that "the end justifies the means." The philosophic precipitate of this sentiment is the doctrine that final causes are primary and paramount. Ends, standards, ideals—so, if they had the language, the doctors of this sentiment would profess—denote a persistent cybernesis, nourished by a continuous feedback which steers and shapes the course of homeostatic events in such wise that their future is at once prevision and providence. This being the case, the future exists and acts before it happens; it is the foregone conclusion of the sequences which it simultaneously forms, guides, and consummates within its all-comprehending span. Past and present then must needs be secondary formations, though aspects of the future's instancy; they are happenings due to and deriving from the inevitable future, their force and form exist solely as means to the future as end. Compared with this perduring end, the means are viable, transitory and perishing. They are the sequence of fancies, visions, inventions, discoveries, alterations, together with their signs and symbols as they arise and lapse. The uses to which they are put contain and spend their entire meaning. They can be employed or laid aside, until they are either discarded for some tool fitted to do their job better, or are used up. Whatever the field, means come, means go; ends go on forever.

Ends are reality. Ends form a system or hierarchy ultimately one, eternal, universal. Our diverse transitory,
concrete, moral and cultural economies, our religious
establishments, and our scientific undertakings, as well
we by our personal histories, only pursue and more or less
exemplify this one, eternal, universal hierarchy of ends.

But, as recorded, the history of means is a history
of competitions with their eliminations and replacements;
the history of ends is a history of conquest, accumulation,
and monopoly. The history of both is a history of war
with strange interludes of peace. Nominate the ends as
you like: "happiness," "salvation," "duty," "power," "self-
realization," "progress," "liberty," "security"—each name
signifies a rule of living and a way of life; each gathers
its relevant literature of dogma and apologetics. Persons
committed to any pursue it under conditions of conflict
with the aficionados of the others, seeking their defeat
and submission, whether in the war of words or of
weapons.

Each end, let it be remembered, is one pattern of
men's struggle to go on struggling, thus first and last a
mutant in the ongoing mutations of liberty. Let it be
likewise remembered that liberty is a verb and not a
noun; that it signalizes the compenetration of a multitude
of quanta; that each quantum is a protean drop of duration whose inward sequences come to pass like the
segregated stills of a motion-picture; that like the latter,
quanta successively flow together into the single image
of the passing event, each quantum an impulsion and
tool advancing its eventuation. And what else can means
or function here be, if not existence? And what else can
existence be, if not both perduing differentiation and
compenetration of the differentiates, if not their identifica-

tion into a same? Taken together, passing one into the other, the differentiates are the passage itself, the transforming transit of past into future as future supervenes, unpredictably other than its past. From initiation until consummation, from birth to death, the passage is end compounding itself of its means, the means being not only used but used up in the end. So food is used up in the feeder, becoming that which feeds upon it. Hence, the ancient insight, that no man can be said to have been happy until he is dead, can apply as aptly to his salvation, to his self-realization, and to any other ideal which directs and impatterns his personal history, except his freedom. For clearly, freedom is the matrix and maturation of all the others. In the last analysis, the years of a life and the events of the years at any moment of the life's history are all the substance the moment can evince. Tradition's dialectic notwithstanding, they cannot be external to it.

True, the dialectic segregates means and ends, artificially isolates them from one another, thus ordaining a metaphysical dualism. But we do not experience them isolated whether in human nature or nature; in art and nature both, means are internal to ends; they generate and constitute the ends they are means to. As the sequential compenetration of works is the ongoing proof of faith, so the successful compounding of means is the consummation of ends. Since ends are ideals, it is the actualization of ideals. No actual end or ideal, hence, can be sovereign and independent, master of the means and unaffected by them. It is recognized that some ends are their own means. But in fact means are internal to ends even when the latter occasion their instrumental existence. The tradition's analysis is an oversight which intends by "means" the residues of use, instead of the substances used up. If this intention were valid, no knife would ever be dulled by cutting, no chair worn by sitting, no food transformed by eating, no road-map affected by passage over the road it maps. Means are operative in the ends which they effect; the ends are their consequences, not their causes, and are generated and constituted as their configuration. The means can exist without the ends, while the ends can neither be created nor exist uncreate except through or in their means.

6. Ideals as Tensions Between the Wisdom of the Body and the Wisdom of the Mind

True, the "realm of ends" of the great tradition is assigned this independence from and sovereignty over actual experience. True, actual experience is reduced to the servile, although often rebellious, status of a recalcitrant dependent on "the realm of ends" said to antecede means, to command them, to discard them. Tradition's transvaluations here are among the consequences of the divergence of the wisdom of the mind from the wisdom of the body; they express the pseudopodic extension of the psychophysical organism's psychic organ's endeavors permanently to redress the perennial imbalance of the organism's struggle to get and keep itself in balance.

The matrix of the divergence is a confusion of desire with the causes of whatever satisfies desire: it is what would be the case if the dogma, *esse est percipi,* were carried over into such maxims as *food is hunger, fire is wanting warmth.* Recent usage calls this "wish-thinking." The dialectic of the tradition has worked it up into the conception that the existence of a wish necessitates the existence of its object, and that the object either creates the wish or the wish the object, a la Pascal's God reassuring the lost stray: "Console thyself, thou would'st not seek me if thou hadst not found me."

Cases do occur when one or the other sequence is an event of experience. Such an event, once realized, then remembered, becomes a design or project of the mind which it can work out consequentially. But the success of the working is never more than a probability, ever an uncertainty, a contingency, subject to thwarting, failure, and frustration. It is the latter as aggregated and compounded in facts, and it is the termination of all workings by death, which the wisdom of the mind compensates for in idea. The idea is born as the mind projects itself to countervail the imbalances which the wisdom of the body does not recover from. It therein constructs absolutes of value out of images, words, and other symbols. Not only are these absolutes never experienced except as those events of consciousness, they also devalue all else that is experienced into unreality and nothingness. Their devaluation involves the endlessly varying compromises of vision and action which the manifold religions and philosophies of mankind embody. But at long last every "realm of ends" is diversely imagined as one, eternal, universal Spirit, indivisibly right and good true and beautiful, the *terminus a quo* and the *terminus ad quem* of the multitudinous, segregated, wrong, erring, evil, mistaken, unbeautiful but immortal human souls, born into the changes and chances of a passing world only to die out of them as they anxiously and knowingly or unknowingly quest for that ever-hidden yet darkly remembered ecstasy which birth has shut them away from.

The perceptual initiation of this eschatologists' ultimacy would seem to be some act of aversion from a present hurt or frustration. The turning-from would seem to evoke and channel itself in some recollection of satisfying unchecked propulsion making a path of determination into an indeterminate future, new-lighting that persistent darkness with the dim flame of a remembered seeing. What is existent, individual, "real" is the felt actuality *from* which the mind turns. That *to* which it turns is at first nothing positive, specific, or creative, unless it be the experience of turning itself. All of it is signified by the words "away," "from." Away "where," away "to" what, makes itself sequentially; this seems to enter perception as a decision of the mind alone, not as a transaction between the whole person and his surroundings. That is, the mind experiences whatever formation ensues as an ideal, an end, with its direction and content a function of the self-preserving organism's avertive activities. The role of this experience as ideal is to preserve, to sustain. Its "absoluteness" is a function of the preservative activities. When such an ideal is given articulation in philosophic discourse, impatterned in a dialectic where a premise is revolved into its foregone conclusion, the perception of that revolution is proclaimed "the" experience of the ideal. Beyond it again is the dark void of the imprevisable, unpredictable future, which *is* truly future only as its passage is a process of variation and innovation beyond forecast, fortune-telling, or prophecy. Thus, the ideal, the value-system, is like a bridge whose base is here and now and whose other end is Utopia, or if you will, nowhere; or it is like the Fakir's rope which his apprentice climbs until he ends as nothing.

7. Ideals Absolute and non-Absolute: Their Roles in Experience

Different cultures and different ages of the same culture build their bridges and braid their ropes of different stuffs. The peoples of India, of China, of Russia, of Araby, of Israel, of Europe, or of the Americas devise and reshape their value-systems from the singularities of vision, action, and speech of their separate collective histories. None long refrains from claiming universal validity for its own "realm of ends," from denying any validity whatsoever to the different ones, and from demanding the conformation of the different with their own. Two modes of attaining conformation are of record. One is to invite others to test the believer's claims for his value-system by studying and working it, and judging the claims on the system's performance in fair and free competition with its alternatives and rivals doing the same job. The other mode applies preponderant force. It refuses competition, penalizes or destroys dissent, and exacts assent.

Neither method follows from what the ideals are. Either way of effecting conformation may be pursued, whatever the ideal. An ideal's status as an absolute whose validity is independent of its instruments and unrelated to its consequence is no more absolute than anything else. Absolute and non-absolute differ not by what they are believed to be, but by the bearing on life and death which their aficionados attribute to them. It is by this bearing that they become objects which our arts exalt, laugh at, or weep over.

Non-absolutes are confirmed, denied, or rendered doubtful through their consequences to life: whether they progressively contribute to rendering it more diversely abundant. Absolutes cannot be so confirmed, denied, or rendered doubtful. They can be validated only in the life lived after death, in the survival of the extinct. For any man alive and not also dead, an absolute ideal's confirmation proceeds with and from his faith in it and his power to exact assent and penalize dissent. Not the character and energy of his absolute but his own will and work are the *de facto* forces of decision. So, men's bitterest wars continue to be wars over value-systems whose validity on merit we cannot establish while we are in fact alive. Establishment must be postponed to the life which belief bets we will live when we are dead. Validation on earth brings those absolutes back from the realms beyond experience to the actualities of experience. And by their works do we know them there.

As the tale of mankind's idealisms ·is told, the experience of ideals is neither itself an absolute nor an awareness of some absolute other than itself. It is an event in the life-stream of events where others regularly precede and still others follow, where occasionally others go alongside. We become aware of ideals when an exigency supervenes, when direction and goal diversify and experience enacts a choosing between divergent ways and ends. In such situations, propulsive awareness heightens, until the intensification reaches its climax as an act of choice and decision. That which is chosen is thereby an ideal, toned by compenetrating anticipation and apprehension and intuited as somehow a revelation-not-to-be-denied. Consciousness supervenes as orchestration of acute momentous tensions between the varied propensities of the enduring manifold whence bourgeon personal and interpersonal history. It signalizes their conciliation and union. Often the tension stretches between unconscious processes of routine, habit, custom, tradition and divergent conscious impulsion. In relation to the latter, the former is moluscullarly inert; it not only doesn't itself change, it pulls against change by others. It manifests a dynamic of inhibition and drag. Where this is overcome, unconscious inertia is transposed into conscious lag, passive resistance into an active ideal which is intuited as a vision of the status quo that action must keep from being altered, either altogether or as little as possible. The limits of visions with such functions are denoted by words like "immortal," "eternal," "universal," "one."

Inasmuch as no man experiences inertia or tradition as unchanging being, inasmuch as every man who remembers the events he lives up, experiences them as cumulative becoming, the rôle of ideals which transpose inertia or tradition from unconscious remembrance to conscious vision is spontaneously compensatory. Ideals so functioning do not put an end to the sequence of diversifications from which the mind would avert; but they compensate in the idea of "End" for the diversifications going on unendingly.

Repeatedly the process of diversification itself brings formations that we do not accept. Their substance disturbs us, or their tempo—they may feel too slow or too fast. Sometimes we want to alter both. Ideals that supervene on such experiences envision divergent formations, altered tempos, newer materials, so orchestrated as to install and sustain a smooth continuation of the personal or interpersonal equilibrations. Ideals that come thus, and for these reasons, do not separate from the mobile actuality, they do not compensate its imbalance; they compenetrate the mobiles and steer, new-channel, and new-shape them from within. Their function is programmatic. Their consequences are new insights, new matters, new media wherein life diversifies and wherewith life advances. Programmatic ideals seem to figure as turning-points in the trajectories of progress, as initiations in idea of *de facto* change and development. Their rôle in mankind's struggle to go on struggling is consequentially more reassuring, but consequentially far less positive than that of the compensatory ideals. The static monism, eternalism, and universalism of the latter seem to go, in history, with a chaotically mobile social anarchy; they accompany a pervasive actual impermanence, insecurity, and hunger signalizing the entire aggregate of interpersonal and intergroup relations. Such, at least, was the pattern which the ideal made with the actual during the ages of faith, so called. The ideal—*vide* Dante or Aquinas—was a well-ordered, articulate depiction of harmony and happiness; the actual was not far from the well-known war of all against all, with preponderant force the arbiter of good and evil, right and wrong: the ideal only compensated the actual; it delineated an otherworld, redressing the imbalance of this world, and thus serving only to accentuate, instead of correcting, the actual imbalances.

Correction seems to be almost exclusively the consequence of ideals employed programmatically. When so used, our ideals do not purport to intend anything forever beyond experience. They operate without illusion and operate within. The kind, range, and degree of alteration they design is postulated upon the gap between things-as-they-are and things-as-we-want-them-to-be, the gap between desire and satisfaction, aspiration and attainment, that must be closed. Programmatic ideals define the closure by defining the ways and works of closure.

Sometimes, on the whole very rarely, the gap is so small that the future we crave need be no more than perduration of the present we possess but which fails while we possess it—the present we would cry unto, like Faust, *Verweile doch, du bist so schön*. The image of self and world which the ideal embodies presents little or nothing to change in order that we may preserve it. There are only its passage and contraction toward nothingness to arrest, and its wholeness to restore where it crumbles. Feature and form suffice as they are perceived. The actual and the ideal are consistent and harmonious. The ideal is representative, the actual satisfies. When this happens, we struggle to maintain the condition, that the latter shall not alter, and the former not blur. When this happens, our experience of the ideal and our experience of the actual come as one continuing pulse of consciousness; the ideal is perceived as an image of the actual, as a projection of the present as future, and the function of the ideal is expressive. The future which the ideal designs prolongs the present, grows out of it with no intended alteration of matter, medium, tempo, or direction; we feel it right and good that what will be shall continue what is, as unchanged as maybe.

8. Every Ideal Can Play All the Roles

Expressive ideals occur infrequently. Alike in the individual life and in the lives of societies, the gap between the actual and the desired, between *is* and *ought-to-be*, is too deep and too wide. Ideals being designs and projections of the desired, they depict the desiderate *what*.

How the *what* is given satisfactory embodiment does not follow from its make-up. The functions of ideals are external to their natures, which are able to assume all and drop all. Which rôle an ideal plays at any occasion, time, or place is incident to chance and change. The same ideal may serve expressively in one situation, compensatorily in another, programmatically in a third. It may at the same time function as compensation for one individual or communion, as program for others, and be appraised as vital lie and delusion by still others. The ideals celebrated by the great tradition have been predominantly compensatory. Only since the Renaissance has their rôle as programs come into the foreground of Western man's attention, and now this rôle, even when it is expressive, relates to the meanings of "is," "ought" and "as if."

We have learned at long last that all the rôles which ideals can assume call for stabilizing and steering an unstable and undirected organism in need of such stability and direction as will keep it going in a circumambience of indifferent and uncharted goings-on. All ideals, whatever their rôles, signalize a transaction between human beings struggling to go on struggling and the chanceful, changing aggregate surrounding them. The common function of all rôles that an ideal may play is preservative: it is somehow to prolong organic survival, somehow to unite in peace warring impulses within, somehow to overcome and to fit to pacific use aggressions and obstructions without. When our propensities launch us on many centrifugal ways toward tangent ends, paralyzing action and making of consciousness a whirl of tensions, there regularly ensues, within certain variable limits, a mode of feedback which brings the divergents to one or another patterned concurrence. Beyond these limits, the psychophysical whole undergoes ruptures, from strokes to psychoses; within them, a variety of centripetal configurations is possible, each a design of means consummating as an end. This, as it forms, discharges psychophysical tensions into an awareness whose content is a flow of concordant images, ideas, and symbols. For this discharge, the awareness and ideal are interchangeable terms. Its eventuation arrests and redirects the trends to fragmentation. It conserves the individual's psychophysical wholeness by putting it on new ways toward a new goal; it liberates liberty from termination.

If the menace comes, not from inner discord but from outer resistance, so that our propulsions penetrate or override environmental barriers, which hold them back and dam them up, an analogous salvation by idealization may ensue. For the dammed up energies then gather tension, the tension mounts until at last it explodes. We usually call the explosions anger, rage, lust, terror, desperation; occasionally we signalize them as joy or ecstasy. As ideo-motor formations, all such outbursts of feeling are literal ecstasies. The psychic propulsions break through, and the personality is said to be "blinded by emotion," "rapt," "out of its mind," "beside itself," "mad." The break-throughs ensue without order, without direction. They are the existentialist's reals, indeterminate and senseless, truly blind, deaf, and dumb to meanings, shaped to no end and articulated by no means. Like all the explosions that nature abounds in, they simply release and dissipate autonomously different energies which have gotten crowded and pressed together beyond endurance. The opening of exits to some may render the pressures endurable to the rest. Then the crowd may become habituated to the crowding. The crowding may stabilize into a sequential pattern of togetherness. This is the sort of thing that occasionally happens on roads without traffic signals or rules. Drivers spontaneously change their unordered movements into an ordered pattern they believe will sustain the free and safe transit of their vehicles. The reordering turns a crowd into a procession. It so mitigates reciprocal delay, arrest, and repulsion, it so smooths and harmonizes movements, as to abolish the condition wherein tensions crowd and press against one another until they can endure no more and explode. Here again the ideal liberates liberty from putting an end to liberty.

Human ideals would seem to be among the inventions wherewith the species keep themselves similarly going without bursting. An individual or collective self's ideals are its agencies of self-preservation. This is how and why ideals are the essentials of spirit. They might be called the steam that the organism lets off as whistlings so that its boilers may keep boiling without blowing up. We note them in history as equilibrators, as releasers, as catalyzers, as channels, and as regulators of the flow of instinct and passion, as directors and shapers of the flow. We note them keeping intact the cycle of homeostatic change wherewith the psychophysical individual consequentially sustains both his organic internal equilibrium and its external transactional balance, and lives on. The arts, the sciences, the discourse of philosophies, the rites and rotes of the religions thus project the ideals of societies. We call such projections a society's cultures, its spirit manifest. History selects from their sequences, impatterns and appraises the selections, and composes them into images of the human enterprise, carrying on.

9. "Living," Actual and Hypostatic: Ideals as Discourse

When the internal and external equilibria are aptly orchestrated to one another, each supporting and supported by the other, human life may be called, as George Santayana called it, the life of reason. Perhaps unhappily, "reason" is a portmanteau word; it packs multiple meanings. Of the many it conveys, two predominate. They keep recurring like hardy perennials. Their disparate exfoliations are denoted by such pairs as wisdom and knowledge, intelligence and intellect, practice and theory, emotion or will and understanding, poetry and science, reasonableness and rationality. The meanings both diverge and overlap, but it is their divergence which counts. By and large, wisdom, intelligence, practice, will, feeling, poetry, and reasonableness go with the actualities of our total struggle to keep on struggling. It is for these that "living" could be the commonest inclusive term. They point to what we do and how we do it as we go on working and fighting in order to change the ambient prohibitions, stoppages, and repulsions which surround us. We strive to change them into formations that should nourish and facilitate freer and more abundant functioning of our powers in that unceasing endeavor to enhance our interests or "values" which renders concrete the pursuit of liberty. "Living," first and last, is our own humanization of the non-human; it is our own specific reformation of the inertia, the indifference, the antagonism, the destructiveness of so much of human and non-human nature into values of our own survival. "Living" is a transaction, between ourselves and the world around, designing and pursuing human advantage as we envision it in ourselves. The vision may range from a solipsist universe

to the barest animal survival. It may aspire simply not
to die.* But this is an exception; only a bona fide solipsism
is rarer. As a rule, "living" is idealization. It consists of an
expanding personal or collective history designing itself
and creating itself according to design by dint of the
individual or group struggle to stay alive; recall suicidal
William James's: "I will posit life in the self-governing
resistance of the ego to the world. Life shall be built in
doing and suffering and creating." In the nature of
things, such creations are no *totum simuls*. They grow
piecemeal, as time pulses, from next to next of concrete
singular event to concrete singular event, trying all things
and cleaving to those which are consequentially trustworthy. Every so often one or another gets exalted above
its peers into an Absolute Truth or Goodness or Beauty
or Right, or into a One which is all of them indistinguish-
ably together, eternal and universal.

Such exaltations—"hypostases" would be the tech-
nical word for the occurrences—are performances of discourse. Discourse is a spontaneous variation in *genus
humanum*, a trait of its singularity and an agency of its
struggle for existence. Its paramount function, communication, still is to nourish and facilitate survival as the
pursuit of freedom. True, discourse can be soliloquy as
well as communication and quite likely always begins as
soliloquy, not *sotto voce*, but with loud outcries such as

---

* *Cf.*: Dostoefsky, in *Crime and Punishment*:
  Where is it I've read that someone condemned to death says or thinks,
  an hour before his death, that if he had to live on some high rock, on
  such a narrow ledge that he'd only room to stand, and the ocean, everlasting darkness, everlasting solitude, everlasting tempest around him,
  if he had to remain standing on a square yard of space all his life, a
  thousand years, eternity, it were better to live so than to die at once!
  Only to live, to live and live! Life, whatever it may be!

babies and animals are given to, especially when suffering
wants unsatisfied, hurts unremedied. These outcries might
be appraised rudimentary ideals; ideals not yet articulate,
compensating, via different organs working on a different
medium, for actualities which the crier is helpless to
better or replace with the relevant organs. But when the
cries more or less regularly bring aid and comfort *ad hoc*,
the cathartic and compensatory function of the soliloquy
is supplemented, and ultimately submerged, by the programmatic one of the communication. Saying and reply-
ing become transactions whence ensue alterations of the
goods, services, and ways of "living." These are at once
creative and destructive. As their transactions continue,
the signs and symbols employed by the communicants
lose old meanings and gain new ones. The process is
sequential, and languages are made up of sequential formations whose birth and death usage registers. Histories
of language recount the patterns of an ongoing rivalry
between the unconscious and gradual change called tradition and the conscious, more sudden changes which we
call innovation. Often a turning point in the never-ending
struggle is an ideal dictionary where meanings should be
so pinned down that they are always and everywhere
this-and-nothing-else, and cannot ever vary from this-
and-nothing-else. Such a dictionary is the ideal to which
schools of philosophical analysis diversely aspire.

One mistaken consequence of their sisyphean struggle
is the doctrine that victory may be won by separating
intent both from the icons which embody it and the
living person's mind that intends it; and again, by separating icon and mind from one another and then hypostat-
izing the intent. The doctrine affirms that intent is
thereby rendered sovereign and independent, and capable

of being reliably grasped one and the same, always and everywhere.

Thence a fiction ensues. It is a hierarchy constructed of thus consecrated "universals," "laws," and other entities, addressed together to a corresponding sequence of profane and perishing particulars. The fiction is sometimes known as philosophic realism, sometimes as logical atomism. It pertains also to what is called phenomenology. Could it be verified in actuality, walking would turn out a universal independent of the limbs and muscles of walkers, talking a universal independent of the chest and voice-box of talkers; and every sequence would be a transit separate from and tangent to the compenetrating events of its trajectory. Actually, words and all other surrogates, however combined and whatever they signify, occur as deployments of psychophysical attitudes and postures in a perceptual transaction. When beginning, they inform unformed discharging organic tensions, thus distinguishing without isolating their compenetrated push, flow, directions, consummations; they articulate them with one another. Grammar and meaning (as the felt relation of sign to significance) together signalize the workings and ways of discourse.

Usually the *terminus a quo* and the *terminus ad quem* of any succession of symbols are the singular concrete events which occasion their formation and use. Once given lasting existence, however, the symbols sustain a certain independence. They become the most durable and subtle components of a mind's milieu, and the most intimate of the overt influences on the human condition; mankind's most man-made and most extensively used media of their transactions with one another. "Discourse" is but one name for such transactions.

10. Discourse of Reason, or Logic, as Ideal

Of recent years, interpreters have been distinguishing discourse as "logical" and as "prelogical," "alogical," "organic." But the conventional measure of its aptness and rightness has remained "logic." Philosophers, theologians, men of science, and mathematicians are presumed to discourse "logically"; while to poets everywhere, to the sages of the far and near East, and to the prophets and rabbis of ancient Israel including the Jesus of the Gospels, interpreters now allow an alogical or pre- or post-logical mode of discourse. Its expressive instances are drawn from the speech of primitive peoples; but it is also variously illustrated, by sports writers and other essayists, from the communications of everyman's daily life. Perhaps its literary apex is currently the prose of the late James Joyce. No disposition is yet manifest to exalt it, to take this for a principle and plan of communication, to envision it as an ideal.

The ideal of discourse, at least in the West, stays "logical." If, on rare occasions, a sage like Emerson may declare consistency the bugaboo of little minds, the intellectual elite are accustomed to adore consistency as a jewel, to assign it maximal survival-value, if not for the cultivator of consistency, then for his neighbor. Their conventions join inconsistency and self-contradiction to error, to hypocrisy, to stupidity and intent to deceive. Discourse, to them, achieves communication and validity in its form and structure, not its flow and function; flow must be consequent on form, function must follow from structure. They cannot endure "mixed metaphors," however simple their meaning. They talk their thinking as if the orders of their utterance and of that which their

utterance conveys are varied modes of repeating identities—not identities as we perceive identities: specific, concrete; each different from the others; interacting with
them; changing as it interacts; mixing in and up yet
sustaining its singularity. No: the identities postulated by
logic are abstractions from such singulars; they are repetitions mysteriously referred to a universal and eternal
oneness of them, which gets disclosed by liquidating
whatever makes their respective uniquenesses, as Socrates'
mortality is made the same as Everyman's by nullifying
in it all the compenetrated differences of persons, places,
times, occasions, circumstances that render the death of
Socrates the unique event it was. Uniquenesses are each
reduced to passing instances of a permament one and
nothing else besides. The perceptual span of their presence
is shut out and cut off. The universals we use in discourse
must be such as neither to change of themselves within,
nor suffer change by any sort of impact from without.
They must be identities isolate and impenetrable, ineffably
this-and-no-other. They are what "the laws of logic"
sustain and police for us.

As employed, these laws are not descriptions of
actuality. They are ideals for actuality, prescriptions for
holding the sameness of some experience unbreached
by inner alteration and outer penetration. Conceptions
must be immaculate. The law of identity, the law of
contradiction, the law of excluded middle realize the
same design and are worked to the same end—to keep
an identity intact, by shutting out what will not stand
together with it and support it, by keeping it pure from
all difference, or by so treating difference as to liquidate
it in the intended sameness. This sameness is thereby
crowned, or, if you like elected, a value whose existence

we struggle for. The "laws" of contradiction, of excluded middle, likewise of sufficient reason, would be futilities save as barriers against an unceasing formation of middles whose exclusion becomes a defensive need; against the bombardment of differences whose contradictions must be nullified, or at least mollified. In discourse, an identity whose survival the laws of logic would serve usually has for setting that experience of defeated effort to penetrate which "the law" of impenetrability points to;* that is, the observation that "two bodies cannot occupy the same space at the same time."

Transposed to the stream of consciousness, it becomes, "two thoughts, hence, should not occupy the same state of mind at the same time." Since, however, mind is a flow of minding in waves of awareness, no state of mind arises as a pure static *now* which follows no *before* nor is succeeded by any *after*. Every intent obtains as a discrete stretch between compenetrating *then* and *soon*. Paying attention to any is endeavoring to cut off and shut out its *then* and *soon,* or to detain them both in its ongoing *now*. The endeavor patterns "state" from "flow." It sequentially designs a complex whole out of parts which it so orders that their configuration permits one and only one place for each; that hence, *what* any part is, and *how* it is joined to the other parts, become foregone conclusions from *what* the whole is. With rare exceptions, all schools of philosophy or psychology rely on logic as an explication of such implications, as a patterned repetition of identicals. Hegelian schools are not among the exceptions, for they hypostatize negativity. They explicate

---

* Data of modern physics render this "law" ambiguous. Field theory can do without it.

"the idea" or "matter" as a repetition of negativity in a set sequence they call "dialectic," whereby everything is rendered identical with everything else as the necessary consequence of an absolute which eternally *is* its own eternal and universal other.

In sum, the discourse of reason, as philosophy, theology, mathematics, or systematic science, is a dialectic of illation, mostly, of course, without benefit of Hegel. The ideal of rationality delineates a patterned whole of clear and distinct ideas each implying the others and consistently explicating the whole. The pattern is hierarchial, the whole being "universal," premise, principle; the parts being inferences, foregone conclusions. Implication is taken for an "internal" relation in virtue of which the parts are members of one another, "consistent" with one another, "coherent" with one another, and following from their whole. Consistency, coherence, implication, denote consummations or ends of the repetitions of sames to which the laws of thought are means. They affirm the primal identity and channel and shape its repetitions to their confirming termination. The termination is a "system."

To experience this consequence of repetition in any milieu is to perceive an actual configuration of symbols, signs, and other icons which relate to different actualities as ideal relates to event. When we experience "rationality" in any discourse of reason, we in fact experience an ideal playing an expressive, compensatory, or programmatic rôle in our transactions with the residual milieu. That "feeling of the sufficiency of the present moment" which William James signalizes as "the sentiment of rationality" is its perceptual initiation. The logic of discourse is the design for the endeavor to win back this sufficiency after it has lapsed, or to recreate if not renew it when its lack is felt.

11. Freedom, Alogical Discourse, and the "Concrete Universal" in the Designing of Ideals

The divergence of the flow of experience into logical and alogical patterns, which discourse prolongs and diversifies, seems, then, a consequence of this felt lack, an effort to supply it. For sufficient present moments do come and we realize them as spans and stretches of compenetrated presences, differing and incongruous with one another as may be, yet together and at peace. They do, somehow, occupy the same place at the same time. Separating them out, isolating each from the others, could render a sufficient present moment singularly insufficent and install a sentiment of irrationality which alone some Hegelian might glorify as reason. Only by a mixed metaphor can we identify the sufficiency of a moment which consummates an ingathering of the dispersed with a system of clear and distinct ideas which *are* clear and distinct only as they are kept segregated. This system, to be a system, must leave out far more than it can take in. Only by mixed metaphor can such a system be taken as a repetition of the original totality. The conceptions of which it is put together are actually residues left over when we strip away from the individual, from the specific and the concrete, the determinateness of its singularity. Universals, as Occam discerned long ago, become indices that can be pointed at multitudes, while in and of themselves they point not even at themselves. Occam called them *flatus vocis*. They are always sound and often fury, to which sense and meanings accrue piecemeal from the singularities of the events amid which they come to function, mostly human beings addressing each other by tongue or pen. When hypostatized into absolutes, into self-sames always different from everything of the kind perceived and yet the identity with one another of everything of the kind perceived, "absolute" is made a surrogate for "indeterminate." Universals then are in effect oracles like those at Delphi or Dodona, previsions of the future which any and every specific event verifies. Whatever happens, no matter how disappointing to expectation, how great its conflict with alternative happenings, believers accept it as validating the oracular universal's intention, fulfilling its prophecy. Since, as experience goes, incommensurable singularities pass over into one another and thereby project a degree of commensurability which creates the universal and renders it the seeing of the past and the prophecy of the future we use it for, we adore it as intellectual intuition and we employ it as the common sign or symbol of those singularities. In terms of any logic, it is both an enduring concretion of illogic, alogic, prelogic, post-logic and the actual ground and goal of logic and of the intellectualisms and rationalisms logic engenders. Each school, by enthroning its own rationalism as the one and only absolute, ineffably both concrete and universal, and thus fencing it off from free consequential inquiry, renders evident how non-rational is the propulsion generating our rationalisms and what gargantuan rationalizations they are *in actu*.

For, in the actualities of discourse, concrete universals are common counters. We experience them as the ongoing formations of consequential reflection, the enduring substance of the non-logical, be the prefix to its logic *pre*, *post*, *a*, or *ill*, or whether we exalt it as "organic thinking." Traditions are ongoing formations of concrete universals. Symbols and myths (this, Plato knew very well) are such formations, more or less finished. They produce, they *are*, the atmospheres, the discernible climates of opinion that bring the discontinuities and isolates of experience together and link them in a union which does not liquidate their specific identities, yet does compound them. They serve to supply body and sanction to a way of life; they support it with a ground and transvalue it with a goal. They are the waves of a culture's predictable future, the insights and agents of the wisdom of its sages and the customs of its folks as the latter jointly and severally struggle for survival. They are the patterns of this survival,* each with its own singularity of works and ways. In their context, consequently, intent is "practical," perception is "poetic," reflection is "intelligence," knowledge is skill, knowhow, wisdom; configurative processes are "reasonable," and all are concurrently repetitive *and* creative. In their context, mind is an ongoing orchestration of feelings and doings whereof a personal or group history builds itself up.

By origin and nature, as by function, these "universals" are ideals, and the experience of them is the perception of ideals *in actu*. They are the ambient greater discourse surrounding the discourse of reason, which diverges amid them as an independent variable, sometimes at their foreground, sometimes on the fringe, and shifts all over the field. In relation to them the rôle of rationalistic discourse varies as culture varies from culture.

---

* *Cf.* B. Malinowski: *Magic, Science and Religion;* M. Kadushin: *Organic Thinking; The Rabbinic Mind.*

In some cultures, logic serves as a confirmer and strengthener, especially of the religious mythos; others use it, as Occam his razor, to cleanse, to purify, to simplify, to establish an order that shall more greatly serve a greater liberty; in still others, logic defines the trigger which should release energies of vision and action that are bound to repetitive inertia by symbol and by myth. In all the discourse of reason, logic is a dynamic agency which, because of its dynamism, also gets itself transvalued into myth and symbol. The act of faith effecting this transvaluation, assuming this tool into an idol, exalting reasoning into reason, and reasonableness into rationality, cannot but be an alogical, prelogical impulsion, a mythopoesis which endows logic with magic abilities beyond any it ever does or can manifest. Nor are the changing ways and works of the sciences, which are styled "the logic of science," exempt from the same idolization and endowment; the uncertainties they make do with get promoted to certainties, and the reliable knowledge they pursue gets enthroned as infallible truth waiting to be envisioned, even as the God of the theologians.

By his act of faith the realist or idealist thus hypostatizes actual logic into a metaphysical power; he denatures it into a supernatural ideal that shall forever insure the victory of the absolutist, whatever his species, in the war where all ideals are weapons for the preservation of the denominations of idealizers.

Does it not follow that faith in reason above all things is thus a choice between alternatives whose moving energy cannot itself be reason? On the record, does not the dominant motive remain freedom; do not the ground and goal of every other ground and goal remain freedom?

Is not reason chosen because it is experienced as freedom's enduringly most reliable instrument of freedom in man's perennial war of liberation?

The old great tradition of the humanities so testifies. And so the newer tradition testifies which grows from the free faith that lives in the works and ways of science. All the sciences and all the arts which this faith engenders, with their signatures in truth or beauty or laughter or tears, also recognize reason as liberty's most reliable weapon and tool in their own struggles to keep on struggling, their own liberty's pursuit of further liberty. And the recognition is most signal—*vide* the argumentation of both the believing and unbelieving existentialists—by those whose passions reason most skillfully against it. To them, too, reason is the differentia of the civilized man, wherever and whatever his civilty be, and whatever and wherever he grows his civilty from.

INDEX